the joy of text

Also by Kristina Grish

Addickted: 12 Steps to Kicking Your Bad Boy Habit
Boy Vey! The Shiksa's Guide to Dating Jewish Men
We Need to Talk. But First, Do You Like My Shoes?

the joy of text

>>mating, dating, and techno-relating

kristina grish

SIMON SPOTLIGHT ENTERTAINMENT
New York | London | Toronto | Sydney

NOTE TO READERS: Some of the names and identifying details of people mentioned in this book have been changed, and some of those mentioned are composite characters.

SSE

SIMON SPOTLIGHT ENTERTAINMENT
An imprint of Simon & Schuster
1230 Avenue of the Americas, New York, New York 10020

Designed by Steve Kennedy
Manufactured in the United States of America
10 9 8 7 6 5 4 3 2
Library of Congress Cataloging-in-Publication Data
Grish, Kristina.
The joy of text / by Kristina Grish.—1st ed.
p. cm.
ISBN-13: 978-1-4169-1897-4
ISBN-10: 1-4169-1897-3
1. Online dating. 2. Dating (Social customs) 3. Interpersonal communication. 4. Text
messages (Telephone systems) 5. Electronic mail messages. 6. Online etiquette. 7. Single
women—Psychology. 8. Single women—Social life and customs—21st century. I. Title.
HQ801.82.G75 007
306.730285—dc22
2006019073

To my dad, with xox

Special thanks to my talented editor Emily Westlake and everyone at Simon Spotlight Entertainment for their faith, enthusiasm, and hard work. Heaps of gratitude to my agent Elisabeth Weed for making this project happen, and to Scott Mebus for his endless support, as well as Alia Malley for her tireless eyes and sardonic dating tales. Alia, you're a rare find and a good friend

>>table of contents

the joy of text

introduction:

>>text and the single girl

ASK ANY GIRL WHAT SHE WANTS FROM A MAN, AND she'll say that beyond diamonds and morning sex, she needs to be understood. We want guys to appreciate us, to listen to us, to just fucking get it—without having to hold their hands as we explain every thought and feeling. We don't have time to spell it all out, and if we do make the effort, our audience had better be captive and worth it.

And as life zooms by, a single girl's revolving-door relationships become the norm—which makes the whole "appreciate-me" deal more complicated than we'd like. Forget biological clocks. Our own schedules make it tricky for us to effectively reach a soul mate's heart. Especially since women live and date in a world where 1) we're busy; 2) guys are busy; and 3) messages get lost in a busy whirlwind of translation—all of which inhibits clear understanding between the sexes. Pair this with scientific data that says men and women speak different dating languages, and our search for a real connection feels more like we're all playing grab-ass in the dark.

Thank Cupid that the Technology Gods have rescued us from mucked-up love lives by inventing so many new ways to help us share what we mean, feel, and want! Or, um, have they? Email, text messages, PDAs, and instant messages intend to better bond our randy global village—and in many cases, they've been successful. And with cash in hand, we've eagerly integrated various channels into our dating repertoire. But herein lies the obvious glitch: We've anxiously done so without a gatekeeper . . . and sometimes in lieu of real-life encounters.

By the time this book lands on your nightstand, infinitely more gadgets will have reared their wireless heads—along with oodles of phone numbers, emails, and IM addresses they've helped reap and store. Who can blame you for getting sucked in? Tech inundation is enough to confuse *and* tickle anyone's libido, since there's something undeniably wild about flirting in a limitless world that lacks rules, boundaries, or watchdogs. But with such mystery comes an unwieldy free-for-all in the techno-relating department. And when you stop to think about it, this means the only dudes who have the ability to piece together our various thoughts and identities are hackers, IT experts, and postmasters who return misdirected or salacious emails.

And I don't even think the last one's a person.

>>move over, miss manners . . .

On any given night, you can have dinner with family, text message tomorrow's date, catch your boss's call, and return quick emails from pals you met online—all within minutes and with little public scorn. Insulting? Um . . . Poor form? Probably. Not that we have any real clue, since even the most primo cell reception can't reach Emily Post for etiquette advice on this one. And when it specifically comes to dating, we've never been told how to properly communicate text, timing, or tone in any new medium. Part of the problem is that once a girl thinks she's perfected the art of intimately connecting via tech, some well-intentioned Brainiac invents cooler, faster, sleeker ways to challenge her MO. It also doesn't help that both sexes are racing ahead with the Brainiac—minus any sense of propriety that might help us fill in emotional gaps.

Enough is enough. In our quest to understand and be understood, *The Joy of Text* will establish hard and fast rules to help you better navigate your love life via technology. Short of an online shopping spree to Agent Provocateur, I can't think of a more powerful way to penetrate a man's multiple channels than to massage his contraptions. The trick is to write with ease, confidence, insight, and more than a little sass. Language is a very powerful force, and when we techno-relate with others, we have the privilege of manipulating it to our advantage. We also have the chance to massively fall short with a slip of the Send button, moments too soon. But tech mishaps are bound to occur; they'll simply happen less frequently once you've finished this book.

Throughout *The Joy of Text*, we'll discuss how to date, mate, and techno-relate with the men of your cyber dreams. Mentally bookmark the following stumpers, which we'll address in future chapters: Should you judge a man by his typos? How do you craft an attractive online profile? Can you spin a mistake? And are booty-call blockers and self-destructing text messages necessary gimmicks—or passing fads, better replaced by good, old fashioned self-restraint?

These are the questions that fry a girl's brain.

>>when your fingers do the talking

Effective communication is as much about listening as it is about talking. This doesn't mean you have to blab over the Internet with Skype to hear someone's voice and pay attention to his words. Listening is about concentrating on language (yours and his)—and how it's used. Specific tech trends will come and go, but once you learn how to behave within and despite these movements, your listening savvy will easily translate to future mediums. Go on, take advantage of text. Words beg to be used, abused, or ignored altogether. You're the one in control of how you techno-relate with others. A virus-free computer and healthy sex drive are simply a means to developing these relationships.

As you know, we live in a world of instant-gratification. People, places, and things demand our constant attention—and wow, do we give it up. And so the logic goes: If bosses and friends insist upon 24/7 accessibility, why can't the boys play too? They can—but be careful not to allow professional and personal habits to overlap in weird ways. Just because you're a genius with one audience doesn't mean you're a pro with another. Practice makes couples. The secret is to match online and off-line communication within context. Here, learn from one of my mistakes.

>>face the facts

When I worked for a high-profile Internet company, my peers and I were squished into a limited loft space. Though we sat shoulder-to-shoulder, everyone used IM as a primary means of communication for quiet and efficiency. Twelve hours a day, I received direction from meticulous supervisors, gossiped with friends who sat within earshot, and doled out instructions to anxious underlings—using abbreviated language, real time, and an oversized screen. I'm not a huge fan of most emoticons, but when I wanted to express apathy or boredom, I often clicked on the familiar yellow face whose tongue wags to the right. Yep, you know the one . . .

Cut to a first date at an overrated Cajun restaurant. I'd been a long-suffering employee all day, but pulled myself together in hopes of a long-pleasuring night. During cocktails, I impressed with animated expressions and name-game banter. Yet when our waitress droned on about specials, I totally zoned out. She stuck around for an appetizer order, so my date asked if I thought the soup sounded good. Instead of responding like a mature, articulate woman, I instinctively made droopy eyelids and slipped my tongue to the side.

"Did you just make an IM face?" he whispered. The man was confused, embarrassed, and more than a bit disgusted by my response. Oops, I said. I guess I did, I said—though it was entirely subconscious. Nobody laughed but me. Soon after our exchange, my date asked for the check—and I never heard from him again.

Alone in bed that night, I couldn't stop thinking about my lame evening. Not because I repulsed my date. Instead, I marveled at the extent to which technology had become such an integral part of my life. Because I spoke to peers and friends all day on IM, the apathy face snuck its way into my off-line vocabulary. My mimicked expression was accidental (and one I never repeated in person), yet the IM icon had, in fact, become a kind of text I used as a substitute for live words. And like any other mode of communication, I realized that successful techno-relating relies heavily on using the right language, at the right place and time. Online and off.

Though *The Joy of Text* will obviously not advise you to mimic emoticons or scream "LOL!" when a wanker invites you back to his pad, it will dispense tips on how to perfect your techno-moxie to build relationships. Consider it a user's manual that helps others understand how you're programmed. You'll also learn how to explain (or explain away) perks and quirks in your personality, intentions, interests, and attitude as you relate with men—while sussing out their best and worst qualities en route. If given the choice, would you ever settle for a slower and less efficient computer, phone, or BlackBerry than your needs command? Of course not! So don't short-circuit your love life either—especially when an upgrade is just pages away.

>>the online meet market

REMEMBER HOW EXCITED YOU WERE THE FIRST TIME you posted your profile on an online dating site? That was in 2003, when the trend was at its popularity peak and the *New York Times* wouldn't stop praising the "Who knew?" success stories. You probably took it pretty seriously, too. Today you have at least five friends who are married or in long-term relationships from pairing their like-minded profiles. And even if you now graze in tech-free pastures, you still know a bevy of singles who subscribe for the hell of it or voyeuristically entertain options with a volley of emails. I mean, who seriously pursues BigJon28 unless he promises a really good time?

More people than you think, actually. According to fans, the major coup of online dating is that it replaces the awkward first step of asking a guy to spell out his interests when you actually meet. And look at that: The info even arrives in a polished marketing pitch, formatted in a predictable grid of photos and one-liners. But while this very major step intends to make that first date easier, it also leaves room for preliminary judgment, skewed expectations, and false pretenses. If you're doubtful about whether online dating is your deal, ask yourself this before logging on: Would you rather figure out a man's best talking points for yourself? Do you think there's something pleasantly mysterious about meeting in person, and *then* deciding whether you're interested? When I think about some of my best dating experiences, I question whether we'd have been drawn to each other on paper. After all, a guy's most adorable qualities are often those he doesn't see in himself—never mind being able to summarize them in 250 words or fewer.

Now this isn't to say that online dating is a total bust, because companies like Match.com and Jdate.com have the numbers to prove otherwise, especially as users get older and hope to settle down. There are approximately ninety million U.S. singles over age eighteen, says the U.S. Census Bureau—and according to a 2005 survey conducted by Match.com, 63 percent of them are open to online dating. Lavalife.com, which claims core users between twenty-five and thirty-four years old, insists that the site's singles trade more than 1.3 million messages a day. With that said, online dating has surely become yet another way to meet singles, and since it's hit mainstream status, this avenue's officially shook its desperation stigma. However, what I find most interesting is that singles who lived, canoodled, and shagged their way through the boom now mix and match their online dating agendas (if they're still logged-on). They're customizing needs—and enjoying every minute.

Look. If you're in the market for a serious relationship, you'll find one online if you search long and hard enough; similarly, if you were in the market for a pair of snakeskin Jimmy Choos, you'd stop at nothing to locate the perfect pair. Determination, repeated attempts, and a whole lot of chutzpah are the foundation for successful online pairing. And while these sites may help people find mates, my hunch is that they don't help them meet more quickly among twenty- to thirtysomethings, who love to reinvent ways to make the Internet work for them. Because online dating is now yet another way—rather than the latest, greatest way—to meet new people, your success rate here is as much of a gamble as it would be with blind dates, work intros, common interest groups, religious functions, and fated happenstance. Online dating has altered the meet-and-greet landscape tremendously—but it certainly doesn't have the cachet it once did, because it's now just part of a greater fold. If you were a fussy dater before the Internet, you'll scrutinize profiles on a page as carefully as you do real people in a bar. If you're a hot floozy with more notches on your belt than Lindsay Lohan, you'll do the same number of men online. If you're a shut-in who never leaves her apartment, your hermitlike instincts will eek out thru hesitant text. My hope is that should you decide to post an online profile, you'll walk the line between wow and real—so there are few surprises and disappointments when and if you finally meet your mate in person.

True compatibility is derived from in-person and online chemistry, as well as shared interests—and by the end of this book, you'll be that much closer to achieving and recognizing each when a great man pops into your life, no matter how you find him. If you're determined to meet a winner online, don't limit yourself to general dating sites. It's my educated guess that those on which you'll most naturally thrive are niche sites that speak to lifestyle, cultural, or religious interests; community sites in which dating is secondary to mingling; and common interest sites that promote face time at club-oriented events. Your image, culture, and hobbies already target those who share your priorities. Compare these scenarios to the difference between shopping at a department store or specialty boutique. We're a culture of customization. If you can find denim shops that sell jeans to compliment your body's curves, you should expect nothing less from dating destinations that flatter your rambunctious love life.

>>what's a girl like you doing on a site like this?

The median ages, interests, funding, acquisitions, ancillary programs, and sheer popularity of dating and community sites are constantly in flux—which is why you're getting the quick and dirty version of the most talked-about venues (at least, as I'm typing this). You don't need me to tell you that public opinion is subject to switch on a dime; both the beauty and the beast of technology is that it's never constant. The Internet is an open forum for change, discussion, and reinvention. This also means that while the following list will tout my opinions about various sites, you don't need to use the venues as they were myopically intended.

For instance: Are you into an indie rocker from Consumating.com, but want your friends to quiz his cred before you agree to a long night of cheap whiskey? Take your conversation onto MySpace.com and share your playlists through iTunes. Want to road test the social skills of a Dungeons & Dragons sexpot on Geek 2 Geek (gk2gk.com) before you're seen together in public? Take it immediately off-line, and meet for a latte under the pretense of exchanging twenty-sided die. If you're not sure whether you're down with the online scene at all, you wouldn't be the first to create multiple aliases with site-specific photos just to learn the types of men you bait—and decide later if you want to nibble back, and how aggressively.

In such an unpredictable dating, mating, and relating culture, the most I can do is tease with a few online options, and leave the process up to you. Think of this meet market as a "Choose Your Own Adventure" tale in which you're the irresistible protagonist who deserves nothing more than a Knight in Shining Plasma. The only thing I ask is that you please approach each experience with discerning judgment and a fair degree of caution, as not every man treats Internet dating with the wide-eyed optimism you do. The last thing I need to hear is that you've been sold to a Kazakhstan moneybucks as his private dancer.

✉ **Consumating.com**: Designed for the international hipster contingent, this dating and community site uses one-word tags versus normie profiles—as the site says, "to identify your interests without having to fit into any rigid stereotype." Daters search profiles by combining tags to create a perfect date, make friends with asymmetrical hair, or tap their inner manic depressive. Weekly questions and a popularity contest shoot for deliberate irony. If I could tag this site, I'd opt for the words "clever," "narcissistic," and "meds-ASAP."

But the design is fun, and if you're in on the jokes, the user experience is so simple that you can't help but want to crash the party.

✉ **Craigslist.com:** Craigslist personals are downright creepy. I know one woman whose ex-boyfriend used them to meet prostitutes, and another whose C-date took her to a peep show and then peed into her empty soda bottle. Find roommates, a wine rack, or an international event here if you must. But a man who isn't a con artist, freak show, or stalker-in-waiting? Not a chance.

✉ **eHarmony.com:** Using his patented Compatibility Matchmaking System™ relationship expert Dr. Neil Clark Warren's site couples men and women based on years of research about what he says will make for a satisfied couple. By the looks of this site, it helps to be attractive, middle-aged, and a fan of dating within your race. You can't argue with success, but you should be serious about settling down. These mature grown-ups are in it for the long haul.

✉ **Friendster.com:** As one of the first community sites to emerge in the midst of the online dating boom, Friendster provides an option for those who want to meet new people, get busy, or both. With over twenty-four million members, you can connect with current friends, make new ones, share info, organize events, find dates, and reconnect with kids from your past (without the hassle of Google and IMDB searches).

Invite chums to join your network; they'll invite their pals, and before you know it, your network will expand to 903,382 "friends" you may never meet. Bonus incentives like classifieds, personal radio stations, blogs, horoscopes, and video and audio elements are a plus. Sharing files, grabbing photos, and making matches encourage constant interaction. Dating is a by-product of the Friendster community, so you look less forlorn trolling for singles here than on a dating site. The coupling option is indirect and thus less stigmatized, plus most members are on it to kill time at work; you might as well try for some action during your nine-to-five.

✉ **gk2gk.com:** That's Geek 2 Geek, for those who traded bottle-cap glasses for contacts. Not that it matters how well you see, since this site doesn't let members post photos. Evidently, geeks don't care about vanity—though they do feel the need to convince visitors as to why they make great partners, thanks to a Top 10 list. If you fetishize socializing loners and giving Trekkies a makeover, these faceless nerds are for you. Then again, if you're out to beam a Captain Kirk look-alike (and who doesn't love William Shatner), Trekpassions.com will meet your needs more specifically. This dating site for sci-fi lovers proves that just about anyone can get laid online. Your biggest threat? If there's a stranger who can hack your Dell, he's hanging here.

✉ **JDate.com:** Mazel tov if you fit the religious/cultural profile! One of the most successful sites on the web, JDate drives home the realities of how niche dating leads to true love. If you're not one of the tribe: Check the unaffiliated box, toast to interfaith dating, and get it on with a mensch.

✉**Makeoutclub.com, Impersonals.com:** When someone says their interests are swim meets and witchcraft, should you take it seriously? Of course not, it's alt-irony again! Makeoutclub speaks to "Indie rock kids, punks, hard-core kids, painters, photographers, writers, musicians, programmers, and record collectors" in a much less commercial sense than MySpace. Create a profile that doubles as your private webpage to list interests, post photos, update your blog, and run your own message board. Meanwhile, Impersonals is still small enough to maintain niche credibility with users. Proceed with caution: When skimming photos on artsy sites, angled and cropped shots could be an aesthetic statement or an effort to conceal cutting scars from angsty teen years.

✉ **Match.com:** With fifteen million members in 240 countries, this site claims that over sixty thousand new singles register a day. In fact, the site estimates that more than two hundred marriages or engagements of members or former members occur each month. Match is a really great starting point for online dating exploits, since it corners the market on mass America. However, this is also why some users consider it the Wonder Bread of matchmaking venues. If you prefer the texture of a complex five-grain in the morning, you might want to spread your blueberry jam elsewhere.

✉ **Meetup.com:** With over two million subscribers, Meetup isn't a dating site. It's a community site that encourages people with like-minded interests to host and attend events in person, which happens to increase the potential for amour. Because you're actively connecting online about off-line interests, your single-minded intentions become secondary. Meetup speaks to everyone: from Burning Man fans in NYC to moms in Palm Beach to graphic designers in the Bay Area.

✉**MySpace.com:** Ideal for discovering new music, posting original shorts, and reading some of the tawdriest blogs on the net. In 2006, the site claimed over fifty million registered profiles and 170,000 new members daily—most of whom design their own pages, upload photos, and link to an extended network of friends. They post videos, artwork, songs, and poetry, and liberally sling flattery and insults in the name of self-expression. The site leans young (25 percent of users are under eighteen)— and unlike Friendster, where dating is a subtle thread, MySpace oozes more raw sexuality than a contagious STD. It's also a happy playground for "influencers." So if you want to score with a trendy kid, get ready to fight off the Cougars who can't help but lick their chops.

✉ **Spring Street Personals:** *Nerve* Personals and *The Onion* Personals fall under this corporate head. Four years ago, Spring Street attracted the likes of literary thinkers with a provocative edge. They still invite pretty faces, but now they also tout cliché monikers and canned profiles. Blogs and networks are a nice, albeit clunky, update. What was once forward is now flat. Or maybe I've read so many euphemisms on the Web that once-clever vocab can't help but sound manufactured.

✉ **True.com:** Did your starter marriage go bust? Still jilted from falling for jailbait? With over six million users nationwide, True's determined to reduce rising divorce rates through verified scientific compatibility testing that stands by its methodology, findings, and algorithms. Yes, algorithms. The site even runs criminal background and marriage screenings on every member!

✍ i could go on . . .

. . . but I'm going to stop before my eyes start to cross. As long as singles have access to a keyboard, there will be more online dating, special interest, community network, and plain old scary hook-up sites than you have time to join between set-ups and chance encounters. Though general sites like Yahoo! Personals and AmericanSingles are effective, your best bet is to target your search with lifestyle priorities, personal interests, and religious/cultural affiliations like JDate or ChristianSingles. Community networks like Facebook and Tribe are bookmark-worthy, too. Recognize what's most important to you in a mate, and then zero in on a site that sends you on the most direct path to finding it. Just because your best friend's banging a drummer on MySpace doesn't mean you'll have the same luck—or even want the same assets from a man. So be confident, strategic, and selective about your needs. The best reason to online date is to preselect an otherwise blind encounter. One girl's tarnished hipster is another's geriatric moneybucks.

>>to thine own profile be true

First things, first. Even if you bombed the verbal portion of your SATs, you'll have to write some variation on a classic profile to online date. And at some level, you'd be a bit dim if you didn't aim to impress. Just be careful, since your first inclination will be to hyperbolize, and the last thing you want is to look like you're trying too hard. Be creative, be upbeat—but above all, be real. Once upon a time, subscribers wrote snazzy headlines with cheesy wordplay to make their profiles stand out. They crafted essays with the skill and time one might devote to a college entrance exam, but with good reason: The online venue was still new. It was the equivalent of hitting the newest nightclub, crawling with singles that couldn't wait to hook up. But just to get past the velvet rope, you were also expected to style a killer look and exhibit serious attitude. You knew that nobody likes a phony, but the real you—the one who'd rather be invited to a low-key dinner party with a gourmet guest chef—was likely hidden under vintage Chloé and Shu Uemura lashes. Now that online dating has become just another way to meet your match, and as community and niche sites double as dating venues, there's no need to flaunt a commercial portrait. Remember that you're writing for an audience, but leave the pomp and circumstance behind.

Remove the Internet detail from the impending romance equation for a minute, and think about the type of person to whom you'd be attracted in real life. My guess is that he's cute, funny, attentive, confident, bright, honest, and a tad vulnerable (among other irresistibles). That said, look for these qualities when you're patrolling the online scene, but more important, exhibit them yourself. Though the forum lends itself to a competitive façade, your goal isn't to win but to meet a like-minded match. Of course you want to snag a man who has fascinating interests, but on a deeper level, you want to meet someone who reminds you of yourself. You want to identify with his voice, style, and intelligence. These are just three subconscious links that sustain a relationship. Being great squash partners will only keep your love alive for so long.

And if you flip this theory, a nice catch won't be drawn to someone who's posing as a souped-up version of herself either. When writing, focus on the traits you love about your person, the environments in which you're most adored—and watch your profile pop among the glitzier riff-raff. A frank synopsis also makes live dates less intimidating, because you won't have to work overtime to live up to an exaggerated personality you'd have otherwise advertised.

>>wait! does this mean mom was right?!?

Usually the adage "Just be yourself" falls flat in the advice department. But the alternative, especially when you're techno-relating, means you'll either spend dates backpedaling to cover fibs or challenged by an exhausting conversation to maintain face. Euch!

When it comes to the online dating shtick, the absolute best you can be is your raw self—especially since that's who your future partner's waiting to meet. Try these ten tricks to maintain a solid online profile and steady techno-relating game that's genuine, attractive, and fluff-free.

⊠ The more substantial your profile, the more substantial your future mate. Be specific when writing essays or answering questions. There's pixie magic in details. It's much more interesting to read: "I tip my hat to the watermelon crawl twice a month," than simply, "I like to dance."

⊠ Make sure you reveal specifics that are most relevant in your life. Sure, any guy would be impressed to read that you ice dive. But the fact that you only went once on a dare, and swore you'd never return to the frigid waters, does not make this a hobby. The story's impressive, but it's more accurate as an anecdote over appetizers than as a preliminary descriptive.

⊠ Write colloquially, as if you're sending your best friend an email. Underscore all facts with plenty of tone; warmth, humor, confidence, and self-deprecation add oomph to your persona. Do not list emotional qualities! Prove them in your writing.

⊠ Be creative, but don't stretch beyond your limits. If you're not a poet, he's gonna know it.

⊠ Watch the TMI: Nobody needs to know about your OCD, string of ex-husbands, or history of bitter layoffs. But if you're more comfortable revealing major vulnerabilities, sooner rather than later, go for it. Having a handicap or being raised in an orphanage qualify as two examples.

✉ Be upbeat, but leave pom-poms at the door. Too much happy is just as gross as too much negativity. Ditto with the snark factor. Let him feel intimidated after he meets you.

✉ Only post photos from the past six months. Grab the digital cam and snap a sweet shot if you don't have one on hand. If you looked sexier two years ago, save the trip down memory lane for your three-month anniversary. How annoyed would you be if your date arrived with more pudge and less hair than he promised? That's blatant lying, and reason to walk after a handshake.

✉ Which reminds me: No matter how shy or self-conscious, don't shoot odd angles or crop indistinguishably unless you work in the art biz. Think of your photo as a visual that accompanies a magazine article; if it can relate to the text, it rounds-out the profile. Just don't skip the picture part. This is the equivalent of wearing a mask to a restaurant, or a paper bag over your head to a speed dating event. Nobody will ask you out—except maybe another photo-free gent. You might as well just go on a blind date; at least when you're set up, you get visual reference points so it's not a total shocker.

✉ As you reel in a gaggle of men, remember that you're after quality, not quantity. Use your initial ego boost from receiving so much attention to write confidently to a few good selects.

I'd keep in touch with three at a time, five at most, depending on how well you juggle. Spread yourself too thin, and you risk giving too much of yourself to one person and not enough to another. Don't worry about your supply running out! There are more Lotharios where these came from.

✉ Finally, I'd wait three solid communication days before agreeing to a date. With so many means of techno-relating on your hands, this timeframe should provide enough instant messages, emails, text messages, etc. to decide who's worth meeting in person—and who's worth leaving behind.

✐ how to speak the same language

So get this. I recently learned that there are three kinds of communicators in this world: auditory, visual, and kinesthetic. Men and women who are auditory focus on listening, visuals concentrate on appearance, and kinesthetics care most about feelings and touch. When you're techno-relating with a man whom you really want to reach, pay attention to how he writes—and mimic his language. If he uses words like "hear" and "sounds" in a sentence, then he's likely auditory. If he uses vocab like "see," "view," or "watch," then he's visual. Kinesthetic men use the words "feel," "hands," and "touch" to get their points across most. The whole shtick starts to become second nature once you get the drift.

As a for-instance, let's say you're planning to hit a movie with your new guy. Depending on his vocab preferences, he might opt for one of the following ways to discuss this:

✉ Auditory: "I *hear* you love Woody Allen films. Interested in his latest?"

✉ Visual: "Want to go *see* an American icon, while he's still in his prime?"

✉ Kinesthetic: "Let's *touch* base later about the movie time . . ."

Obviously, men and women never stick with only one type of speech, but tallying majority use indicates how your guy best communicates, and how your words can most effectively resonate with him. Don't be surprised if a man's not the type you initially suspect. Auditory communicators are a rare find—and although you might assume artists are visual, most are actually kinesthetic. To sculpt or paint, one must be tactile and fueled by emotion to create.

But enough about the dudes! Start weeding through past messages *you've* written to dates or friends. Recognize the language imagery you've used to help you determine your communication forte—and enjoy the sneak peek into one small but important aspect of your techno-relating compatibility. Pairing types isn't a fool-proof plan, but if you can match language, who knows how much deeper you'll connect on other levels too?

>>if your meet goes bad

Hey you, with the furrowed brow. You don't have to like online dating to want to learn how to better techno-relate. If you've tried this avenue and it didn't work, move on to more traditional ways to meet men. You're no worse off than when you began—and you can always circle back after a little hiatus. And if you'd rather chop off your fingertips than use them to craft a profile, then for the love of acrylic tips, stay away from online dating and community sites. By no means do I feel that online dating is a superhighway to a satiating love life, nor is it a prerequisite to following the advice in this book. And that last point is one I'd like to make very clear.

The Joy of Text intends to help women best connect with men via technology—because our modern dating landscape insists upon it. Meeting a wonderful guy online is essentially no different than meeting one (or five) at a gallery or dog park. You're still a gorgeous face in the crowd, and a feisty spirit who has no choice but to ride the ups and downs of a relationship no matter how you initially make contact. I'm just here to help make the process a lot smoother.

>>the (other) elements of style

WHETHER WE'RE TALKING MINISKIRTS OR SEMICOLONS, personal style screams a message to the world about your tastes and values. And more often than not, how this message is interpreted says as much about the sender as it does about the recipient. Style is about preference, which makes both you and your text open to judgment and challenge. It's best to get it right, sooner rather than later.

Remember that when techno-relating, you're building an identity beyond what a person might otherwise see, hear, and feel if you were sitting in the same room. There's no opportunity to gauge vibes, listen to intuition, or interpret body language on either partner's part. That said, your text should really reflect, not reinvent, who you are. I know, I know. Some of the most influential communicators in music, art, and literature ignore traditional rules of composition and rhetoric to create their own sense of brilliance. But just because technology repeatedly provides a blank canvas for text-perimentation, you don't want to cross the line between style and slop. Some of the same great minds that deviated from the basics began with a strong knowledge of them first. So before you invent an insular phonetic code that only you, future boy toys, and Jane Goodall can understand, make sure your inspiration has some foundation in personal truth and external perception—if for no other reason than to use as a platform when defending yourself against snooty recipients. Because believe me, everyone has an opinion on techno-relating . . . and they'll use it to determine your intelligence, coolness, and compatibility. (And so will 735 of their closest friends, if your message becomes part of a forwarded chain.)

Before we dive into the nitty-gritty of stylish do's and don'ts, get to know your audience. This way, you can anticipate how you might specifically address each person and how he might respond. When reading your correspondent, it's important not to make sweeping generalizations about a man's place in the world simply because he boasts specific technologies. If a dapper gent has the newest camera/phone/cappuccino maker combo, don't suppose he's rich, status-conscious, and hyper metrosexual. Men of all ages and incomes love their cargo—and if we used favorite toys to solely nail a guy's persona, a teen with a trust fund might seem no different than a forty-year-old CEO. However, do feel free to make assumptions about types of men-as-professionals and how they most often techno-relate with women. Just watch out for the loopholes. . . .

If you're flirting with a businessman, for example, it's a safe bet that you'll connect most often via BlackBerry, with short messages and a direct tone. Meanwhile, an editor's attentive text messages will sparkle with compliments and word play as if he spent the morning hunched over his phone with bloody thumbs. Comparing the two, it's easy to assume that the editor might be more anxious to meet, have drinks, commit, and have babies. Women love a good talker, and writers sure love to banter! But before you rush to buy monogrammed linens, it's important to first realize that a man's profession can define who he is and how he communicates. His preferred voice and channel are often work-dictated, and his medium of choice becomes as important as his message. In which case, the editor is no more sincere than the businessman simply because one's a wordsmith and the other minces text; in the world of a corporate exec, talk is cheap.

The good news is that you've dated enough guys—or at least watched enough sitcoms—to know that each is built differently. It's when yours is joined at the hip to his best gadget that this cliché takes on a more complex meaning. I said complex, girls. Not impossible.

>>when work becomes foreplay

Because most guys use the same communication channels at work and play, their techno-relating comfort zone will follow suit—especially since so much of your rapport is established while you're on the clock (sorry, Boss Man). Keep in mind: If your guy's a major exec, his rotating assistants have the first-look at notes sent via work email, so write for an audience of two. That

said, here's how your type*—suit or creative—is bound to reach
out, and how he hopes you'll respond.

✉ **Know Your Prospect:** Corporate Slave
  How He Connects: BlackBerry
  What to Expect: Emails and text messages from a man of few
  words. He'll call to confirm dates, if his secretary doesn't reach
  you first. Convince yourself that the phrase "Sent wirelessly via
  BlackBerry from T-Mobile" is a sign of affection. You'll be seeing
  it, lots.
  Don't Neglect: To close emotional deals in person, since
  he's married to his job for now. Mimic word-count when
  corresponding—unless you want to own the platform, since
  you're on a computer and he's tapping away on a mini
  keypad. This is the techno-equivalent to being on top.

✉ **Know Your Prospect:** Media Maven (Editor, Writer,
  Publisher . . .)
  How He Connects: Charming emails and text messages.
  All sweet nothings will mean something; no word or typo is
  accidental. He uses full sentences to cue style: All lowercase
  says he's relaxed, while proper grammar and punctuation
  say he's a stuffy traditionalist.

---

* I obviously can't break down every professional's techno-relating skills; that list would
go on forever, and at some point, you're going to have to do a little work yourself. But
once you study how I skimmed between the pixilated lines above, your ability to read
an audience will become second nature! The secret is to start with a guy's technology
of choice and analyze his actions from there. As if dissecting habits and predicting a
man's behavior are new to you. . . .

What to Expect: A careful proofreader.

Don't Neglect: Measured text! Writing reflects who you are; salutations say how you feel; bad spelling signals stupidity. Sending one-word answers to long diatribes are grounds for The Talk.

✉ **Know Your Prospect:** Advertising Exec

How He Connects: Email, Text, IM, Treo, Facebook, Flickr, MySpace, Second Life . . . you name it. He's in the know about all things nouveau, which he uses to impress new accounts.

What to Expect: Confident, inventive text over various mediums. His pitch will be long, short, flirty, or cerebral— depending on how he plans to strategically target you.

Don't Neglect: To have a gmail.com or mac.com address. Hotmail.com and aol.com are so five years ago. Coded sign-offs in lieu of names read as playful identities.

✉ **Know Your Prospect:** Internet Whiz

How He Connects: Text if he wants to meet, IM if he wants to talk, email if he wants to dump.

What to Expect: He techno-relates on an intimacy hierarchy— from personal email (lowest) to phone call (highest). Sending hidden URLs, cool links, and online games are his version of sending you roses.

Don't Neglect: The possibility of falling in love over IM, even if he sits next to you at work. He can also stalk you like a Manson once you're history, thanks to friends in IT departments. Save naughty gossip and "Can you believe he . . . ?" stories for in-person martini night with friends.

✉ **Know Your Prospect:** Medical Mind

How He Connects: Email or an old-school land line in the operating room.

What to Expect: Become as easy to reach in one place as possible. If you miss his call, you may not hear back for twelve hours. Leave messages with a secretary or nurse; they're his voice mail.

Don't Neglect: To invest in a BlackBerry or Treo, so you're accessible to text messages, emails, and phone calls at all times. Depending on his day, you'll use one (or all) to contact him. This is not pathetic or needy. Sending him the lyrics to Don Johnson's "Heartbeat" over email is—not to mention, it's in questionable taste.

✉ **Know Your Prospect:** Publicity Pusher

How He Connects: Anything from a BlackBerry to a blimp. A PR exec makes sure you know he's hyperbusy but makes time for women who stir his creative juices.

What to Expect: Serious spin on his persona, plus multiple games of tag (phone, text, email, or otherwise). It's in the guy's blood.

Don't Neglect: To challenge him. He's very image-conscious, so know that his witty text has as much to do with impressing himself and your friends as it does with impressing you.

✉ **Know Your Prospect:** Finance Mogul

How He Connects: The Bloomberg System

What to Expect: If you're sent a note with an email address that ends @bloomberg.net, it's official: You've been Bloomberg-ed. Money makers operate on multiple terminals that create an online community for finance types that's kind of like a stock website, email, IM, Friendster, and a very insular Google—all in one. If you work in finance, this is your best techno-relating medium thanks to super high-speed connections. Plus, you can spy on him via his profiles, a chat function, and an open-email alert. If you work in a different industry, this is not the time to play grammar police: He'll bastardize language to its shortest version, because it's his job to transmit info quickly (Think: text message on an email screen). Good with his hands, this one loves to "grab" . . . news from the wire, that is.

Don't Neglect: To seduce the h*ll out of him, since his boss is more likely to read an email sent from his work address than this one. No swearing though, or an email administrator will scold you for inappropriate language. WTF? I guess that's what abbreviations and symbols are for. . . .

✉ **Know Your Prospect:** Artistic Talent

How He Connects: Inventive emails, text messages, camera, and video phones

What to Expect: Original photos and sketches sent via jpeg. Creative text messages like this (. .) will make you blush. In case you're a novice, those are your boobs.

Don't Neglect: To change your IM avatar (the picture on your IM screen) to reflect your mood. Private DV cam movies and naughty phone shots (sans face for safety) speak to his visual core. You can do artsy, too.

✉ **Know Your Prospect:** Legal Eagle
How He Connects: BlackBerry or work email
What to Expect: Email responses from work or BB account within hours; returned messages can take up to two days unless you're willing to field late-night calls. Fifteen-minute rings can be romantic, since privacy isn't an issue with big-office types. Never contact him through a nonwork account like Yahoo, Gmail, Mac, Hotmail, or AOL. Busy attorneys don't have time to check personal accounts very often.
Don't Neglect: To remember that a delayed response may simply reflect a hectic day. When he's on the phone, make plans for late-night weekend dinners. If you reach a dead end with one lawyer, hit the sushi bars open till two a.m. to scope out another. Spicy tuna rolls, with a side of legal ease? Now that's a bedtime snack.

✉ **Know Your Prospect:** Hollywood Mogul
How He Connects: Calls from remote locations. Learn to tolerate spotty cell reception or randomly timed rush jobs when the only phone in the motor home is free. If he really cares, he'll begin his call with the words: "I can't talk now, but in forty-five minutes . . ." Pray for rush-hour traffic.

What to Expect: Put in a first call, but don't count on a response until his team breaks to eat, set up a shot, or move locations—and even then, conversations may come in fifteen-minute bursts.
Don't Neglect: To be patient! Hello, your obvious competition here is movie stars. . . .

✉ **Know Your Prospect:** Unemployed Sap
How He Connects: Just enough calls and text messages to keep you from thinking he's got time to kill. He'll spend most of his minutes watching TV or movies, listening to the radio, downloading songs to his MP3 player, or browsing the Web on his phone.
What to Expect: More action than talk. This booty chaser doesn't have to get up for work. He might as well get it up for you.
Don't Neglect: To take advantage of his hormones, since he'll probably take you on cheap dates. It won't kill you to call in sick, spend the day in bed—and shut off your gadgets, for once.

☎ will he ever just call?

Everyone likes to techno-relate, but I don't know one guy who doesn't appreciate an old-fashioned phone call . . . eventually. Yet because we've learned to covet alternative mediums like IM and email, phone calls have become the Holy Grail of relationships (even if we do screen first). The result? Extensive protocol that prolongs the journey to our very first date. Love it or hate it, the scale inevitably looks like this:

✉ Personal emails: Initiate loose dialogue, and don't question whether he has multiple aliases (especially if you meet online).

Also avoid going too deep on a personal email, because your goal is to graduate to the next level of intimacy. . . .

✉Work email: The address is on his business card—but wait for him to use it first. He checks this address with more frequency than a personal email account, since it forwards directly to his BlackBerry. If you don't mind that his assistant (and ex-assistants) can access this address, send wicked notes during his boring afternoon meetings. Mind your tongue, but don't worry about his watchdog boss. Besides, who knows if you'll be talking to this guy next week?

✉ Instant Message: Sass it up, but make your text match your real personality. Even still, be candid and coy.

✉ Text message: Flirt, play, plan, connect, and say thanks. If brief, then anything goes. No fighting!

✉ Voice mail: Leave a smart but provocative message, and he'll save it. Welcome to his call log.

✉ Phone call: Ding! Ding! You've arrived. Don't abuse the privilege.

✍ hello? is it me you're . . . looking for?

Silly tart. Just because he programmed your digits into his cell when you met doesn't mean he'll use them to call! Once he dials, game's on. Here are a few cues that he's seriously stuck on you:

✉ He assigns a clever ring tone to your number. ("Ain't Too Proud to Beg" is not a compliment.)

✉ He has anytime minutes—and he's not afraid to use them . . . on you.

✉ A shot of your smile or belly button becomes his phone's wallpaper.

✉ You place within his Top 3 speed dials—and you're only outranked by Mom and Hunan Kitchen.

>>can you judge a man by his tpyos?

When it comes to typos, there are two primary schools of thought: 1) Mistakes say you're human; 2) Mistakes say you're stupid. After all, techno-relating grants us the freedom to edit our text—so we can type, delete, re-type . . . and inevitably appear more articulate than we are in person. Unless you're a Mensa candidate, why not take advantage? Even instant messaging, which boasts a real-time exchange and yields only a brief time window to process thoughts, doesn't stop you from editing words en route. The precision with which we're now able to communicate behind a glowing screen is incredible— and for those who are conscientious about their image, the backspace button and spell-check function can be serious godsends.

I use the word "image" above, because that's basically the core of what I'm talking about when prattling on about style: It's the persona that you want your recipient to digest when that IM or email message pops onto his screen. The extent to which we care about another person's mistakes is often dependent upon how much we care about the person—as well as our own pet peeves. But the way I see it, you're better off erring on the side of diligence (or intentional lack thereof); if things work out, you have plenty of time to blow a good impression in real life.

Because acceptable typos are dependent upon the medium, it's easiest to break them down accordingly. We'll stick with the three majors—(email, IM, and text messaging)—because they're the most popular channels and even new tech is simply a variation on their themes. Although techno-relating has negated all excuses for not getting in touch, the mediums haven't yet created ways to stop you from sounding like a GED grad when you do. So hit that spell-check as if a lonely Friday night depends on it. Oh wait a minute, it does.

1. Email: When to Write Someone Off

When it comes to typos, think of emails as modern-day letters. Emails are a personal medium that we expect to be carefully composed before sending, so the less effort you put into one, the more insulting typos become. I'm not the first girl to internalize verbal snafus: If I suspect that a man takes serious time to string together a sentence, he naturally seems more attentive. And attentive equals attractive. Same goes for you, powder puff.

Let's start with spelling. Everyone knows that when chatting with guys, you should write the way you speak, because nobody likes a contrived persona. So if you don't use a thesaurus to talk to men at banks or bars, shelf the fifty-cent words when composing an email. Conversational writing connotes a breezy attitude, so long as you proof for spelling and grammatical typos before hitting Send. To some, mild word snafus are no different than a cough or sneeze—depending on the mistake. My friend Bryan actually makes typos work hard for his cause. He spends an hour crafting genius emails to women he woos—and an additional ten minutes inserting typos: "If the girl's really busy at work or playing hard-to-get, I want to send the impression that I don't have time to proofread my work and that I'm not focusing on her so intensely. I want to give the impression that I just zipped it off."

Bryan squeezes words together, transposes letters or repeats the same letter at the ends of words. He also defies traditional grammar by writing in all lowercase letters for a casual bent. This may sound a bit half-cocked, but you have to admit that Bryan's impression/execution process is well thought out. Of course, there are typos, and then there are typos. Bryan would never use double negatives or type the wrong form of a word, such as "too" instead of "two," or "there" instead of "they're." And neither should you. These mistakes don't say you're relaxed, they say you failed eighth-grade English.

If you're feeling emotional, stream of consciousness run-ons are acceptable when expressing anger or breathless frustration. Otherwise, a lack of commas and periods confuses meaning, tone, and intent. Your response can also read as careless and lazy, and too many run-on sentences send the impression that you don't know when to come up for air. Take that assumption off-line, and nobody likes sipping a 1995 Chateau Margaux with an incessant blabbermouth. Immigrants, foreign exchange students, fashion designers, and artists bend this rule most, thanks to unconventional gaps in their education. Here, the extent to which you wish to play grammar police is up to you.

However! You're given a free pass on abbreviations like "diff" for "different" or "v" for "very"—after you've established a brief email rapport (that's a two-exchange minimum). Abbreviations aren't typos, since they say you're smart enough to sensibly shorten a word for the reader's benefit. Permission to condense words is not to be confused with an allowance to use symbols in an email—"2" should never replace "to," and "R" is not the same as "are." You outgrew such shorthand when you wrote your last letter home from Camp Hiawatha. Colored and cursive fonts evoke the same nausea quotient, unless you're sending a special occasion email like a birthday greeting. If you must get creative, choose one background, color, and script—and stick with it, or risk looking like a kid with a new box of Crayolas. If your email program let you dot letters with hearts and write in bubble font, would you ever embarrass yourself with such saccharine nonsense? Actually, don't answer that.

speaking of email typos

The last thing you want is for your crush's email to resemble one of those spam tests from an erudite but probably bogus source. You know the ones: Every message insists you're a rocket scientist if you can read its gnarled language. I excerpted from an example below, for ref. This one flatters your intellect; others promise years of good fortune.

Unfortunately, such laws do not apply to courtship. A typo-riddled love note forwarded to ten friends doesn't mean you're a whiz-kid with years of luck ahead. It means your friends will tease you for having low standards and the potential to rear obtuse kids with 150 lbs of stupid.

Can you raed tihs? Olny 68 plepoe can.
i cdnuolt blveiee taht I cluod aulaclty uesdnatnrd waht I was rdanieg. The phaonmneal pweor of the hmuan mnid, aoccdrnig to a rscheearch sutdy at Cmabrigde Uinervtisy, it dseno't mtaetr in waht oerdr the ltteres in a wrod are,

the olny iproamtnt tihng is taht the frsit and lsat ltteer be in the rghit pclae. The rset can be a taotl mses and you can sitll raed it whotuit a pboerlm. Tihs is bcuseae the huamn mnid deos not raed ervey lteter by istlef, but the wrod as a wlohe. Azanmig huh? yaeh and I awlyas tghuhot slpeling was ipmorantt! if you can raed tihs forwrad it.

2. Instant Messaging: Fast Girls Finish First

Emails get sucked into a cyberspace void, in which you place a whole lot of faith in your ISP to deliver sentiments on time. But with IM, dealing with typos is the sacrifice we make for instant gratification. Because we talk in real-time, traditional grammar and punctuation rules are often ignored—and in many cases, replaced with new decrees for convenience. Although you might not know how regularly a guy checks his email, IM is a lot like a quick and easy call. Plus, you know when he's logged on, off, at a meeting, at lunch . . . so he's a bit easier to track if need be.

Because you're talking and typing at breakneck speed, typos are a given and abbreviations are a must. Don't bother to correct a misspelled word unless you've muddied its meaning, but do be careful about making grammatical mistakes. Unlike email, your IM partner is told when you're spending too much time typing, thinking, and then backspacing to perfection—which makes it look like you're trying too hard to impress. In any event, never keep your partner waiting longer than three minutes without letting him know when you'll return to the conversation (if ever). There's nothing worse than knowing you've sent a note, noticing a guy's logged on . . . and having no control over whether he intends to write back.

When it comes to punctuation, it's not considered a typo to start a sentence with a lowercase letter and forget to end in a period. And if you don't, you'll not only look like an anal retentive bore but the process will also slow you down. The only person still holding on to capital letters and punctuation marks is your father, who just learned how to log-on. With IM, practical use and etiquette actually follow each other in that order. I'm not suggesting you throw all spelling and punctuation rules out the office window; but I do recommend you pull back. Whether you're on IM or email, the difference between quick and ignorant is still obvious. How you present yourself via tech mediums is like getting dressed for a date. You'd cower at the site of a guy in bad shoes and a stained shirt tucked into his underwear. Similarly, a poorly assembled message is an eye-sore.

But ah, the well-decorated IM is a sight to behold! Because most of us instant message from work, we're multitasking between phone calls, emails, meetings, and even other IMs. And because your hands and mind are in so many places at once, you have license to value speed over mistakes during IM dialogues. What's more, when we use IM to flirt, banter, make plans, and generally play get-to-know-you, it's imperative to add an emotional layer to your techno-relating skills. What's the point of having a little chit-chat, if you can't gauge your partner's reactions to and feelings about your words? Speed plus senti-ment: Here's where the acronym fits in.

Acronyms are not mistakes, but using too many of them can be, because they'll lose their affect. Pepper your favorites throughout an exchange, and avoid those that we love to hate. BRB (be right back); WTF (what the fuck); and BB (bye-bye) are standard raves. When goading your baby, it's natural to strive for the much-appreciated LOL—which is even more special when written in all-caps and followed by an exclamation point. Come to think of it, the only time I'll ever endorse using ALL CAPS or exclamation points is when writing with acronyms on IM. They emphasize fleeting tone—and unlike on email or even a text message, you don't sound in need of anger management courses or a muzzle for your inner cheerleader. More grating acronyms are TTYL (talk to you later), L8R (later), and TTFN (ta-ta for now), which are far too reminiscent of yearbook messages and Trapper Keeper doodles like BFF and TLA. IMHO (in my humble opinion) and PTI (pardon the interruption) are also annoying. If you've written the sentence, your guy knows it's your opinion, and if you're interrupting, you probably don't care about being polite. So stop with the niceties. They look like BS.

When courted by a pseudointellect, I suggest you follow his grammatical lead because he'll be prone to nit-picking verbal minutia. "Spell out the acronyms for God's sake, especially 'K' instead of 'Okay.' I hate that one . . . ," cries my heady peer Josh. "A few extra letters won't hurt, and it makes you sound so much smarter. The purpose of IM is to be quickly conversational, not regress into adolescent nomenclature." Well, then. If you insist on using acronyms but want to play it clever, create your own. This way, you'll develop a system that only you and your partner understand. Mr. Cerebral will like the challenge, and you'll have the chance to out-do his merit.

📖 abbreviate this!

Tired of the same old IM acronyms? Not inspired to craft your own? No worries, I've conjured a few newbies so you don't have to. Spread the word, but take the credit. I won't tell. . . .

BLOS: Boss looking over shoulder

CUBI: Can you believe it?

CL: Call later

CW: Come with

GMAB: Give me a break

GTFO: Get the fuck out

HO: Hung over

L?: Lunch?

LN: Leaving now

NW: No way

OS: One sec

RUF: Are you free (As in: "RUF 2nite?")

SC: So cute

SU: Shut up

TT: Too tired

USMF: You sexy mother . . .

WE: Weekend

3. Text Messaging: Tales from the Cryptic

Tpo? Whts tht? A text message—or txt msg—is all about the intentional typo as a way to jot off a quick hello, idea, or naughty-ism. While some abbreviations borrow from IM verbiage, most are simply phonetic or instinctual. And when writing to parallel the conditions of speech, it's most common to drop out vowels. Believe it or not, a few exchanges are all you need to comprehend a partner's vernacular. And even if friends txt with an accent or crazy hip-hop inflection, your learning curve is short. In this abbreviated forum, txt is understood on a case-by-case basis.

Remember the numbers, symbols, and abbreviations we hated over email and IM? Well, they're now welcome in this format! Feel free to type "2morrow" instead of "tomorrow." Use "ur" instead of "your" or "you're"! With text messaging, top priorities are convenience and precision; scrolling through a keypad for a 160-max word count is a serious pain if you don't abandon your inner schoolmarm. Programs like T9 make techno-relating a bit easier, as do quick notes, but these functions don't guarantee clarity. Text messaging is the very rare instance when inventing your own dictionary is preferred over Webster's. In fact, typos are your friend.

Overly creative text emoticons might look like typos, but these may just be tricky faces to decipher—especially since they rely on a common visual language between sender and recipient. Once it's established, forget the typical smiley face. Make your grin drool, grow a double chin, stick out her tongue, or sport a mustache—if, and only if, you and your guy are like-minded. Which I guess means that in the world of text messaging, the only letter combos that qualify as typos are the twisted result of sending a drunk text. And that conveys a whole other meaning altogether.

✎ when should you return a drunk text?

That would be never—especially if you've been nipping at the bottle yourself. This also means there's no good time to send a drunk text. Because techno-relating already creates instant intimacy, and booze already makes you want to suck face with near-strangers, you'll be passed out in a man's lap before he has time to hail you a cab home. And unlike the booty call, in which your conscience has to talk to (and hear the plea of) a desperate partner, booty texts are sent without a spoken word. Your ears can't cue your conscience about this bad idea, so your judgment is even more impaired. Not to mention, the evidence is permanent . . . and forwardable.

If drunk texts lead to hard-core flirting but no physical connection, the consequences are fewer, and often limited to next-day apologies, likely over text message (again). But keep in mind that major embarrassments here are twofold: 1) They create a disconnect between the online and off-line persona you hope to establish; and 2) They leave a visible record, on both your phone and his, of just how blasted, reckless, and wretched you were the night before. To be entirely honest, I'm not sure which is worse.

>>timing is everything

One of the primary differences between a techno-relating expert and a transparent novice is how well she times her correspondences. This relates to both initiating and responding to a man's effort to make contact. As with any mating dance, you don't want to appear too anxious—but you don't want to let too much time transpire between attempts, either. We've all played the email game in which a guy contacts us, and we wait until four p.m. the next day to return his note. It's as if we're too aloof to make contact before the clock strikes, yet at precisely 3:59 p.m., we rush to the keyboard and finally send the note we saved as a draft just fourteen hours earlier. The thing is, as new tech breakthroughs enter the dating landscape, the four p.m. rule no longer applies, because new gizmos are designed for quick repartee. So what are the latest timelines in our ever-changing, techno-relating climate?

Turnaround time is always relative to how long you've known your sweetheart and how often you two connect. While the four p.m. rule might have worked in the beginning stages of romance, there's never a need to play games once you've laid a solid foundation. Similarly, the following rules revolve around general techno-relating courtesy—but are naturally subject to change based on the back-and-forth you establish with your guy. As with any type of communication, you have a choice as to whether you prefer to ditto someone else's behavior or take the timing lead yourself. Even if he initially reaches out, you can still set an acceptable pace by paralleling online and off-line encounters. When he calculates the timing and number of messages sent, relative to the amount of nookie received, he'll catch on sooner than you think.

So what if your sweetheart uses a limited edition, high-tech device that's not available to the masses until 2020? Or even just the newest Sony import that's yet to hit suburban markets? Don't sweat it. On some level, every mode of technology builds on that which precedes it. And though he's got the gear, you've got the brains; simply match the fundamentals of his gadget's closest sibling with your own instincts on how to techno-relate with style. This will put you in the power seat every time. A safe rule with new and unfamiliar technology: Cut your connection time in half, with each invention. For example, if you usually wait an hour to return a text message, when its sister technology rolls around, volley back in thirty minutes.

1. If It Looks and Reads Like an . . . Email
Because so many men and women have so many different email addresses, days at a time could drift past us before returning a note (and not everyone knows how to import their aliases into their main account). Email demands the least urgent response but allows for the most articulate means of techno-relating. Storytelling, bitching, and long-term planning all lend themselves to this medium because of its hurry-up-and-wait rep. And yes, because we have new and improved ways to techno-relate with our dreamboats, the four p.m. date rule is relatively extinct.

Sniff. Feel free to take a moment.

Feel better? Then kick back, sip a colada, and hope your

email will be answered within a three-day period—and pay those who email you the same courtesy. Anything longer is inexcusable, unless someone's on vacation or a business trip. When it's your turn to respond, try to match and modify length according to a word count that heeds the quickest, most entertaining, and most thorough answers. And should he send a diatribe, and you're tempted to reply with a brief "yes," "no," or "nice," don't bother. Most men I know would rather you not reply at all. "One-word answers or short sentences make me feel used," says my friend Luke. "The girl gets complete entertainment value from me, and I get nothin'."

If your guy's Mr. Monosyllabic, wait two days before considering whether to contact him again. Don't buy the "I'm too busy" implication; he either prefers another mode of communication—in which case, let him contact you—or he's simply blowing you off.

2. If It Looks and Bloopity-Bloops Like an ... Instant Message
This one's a no-brainer, ladies, because timing limits are implied in the medium's name. Don't wait, or let your partner wait, longer than three minutes before returning a message and closing that IM window. If you don't linger for men in real life, you sure aren't tapping your nails over a virtual back-and-forth. Like you, your guy may have multiple windows open at once—but any more than three is disrespectful and likely prophetic of relationship issues to come (Translation: How many relationship options does he keep open? How short is his attention span?).

A promising tip: Employ similar techno-relating techniques

to those used when chatting on the phone. If you sense an awkward conversational pause, are running out of polite fodder, or have the power to leave him sexually on edge, be the first to log off. This is the IM equivalent of hanging up. I don't care if he does have someone at his desk or a call to answer; you want to be his priority. Set the precedent that you don't have time to wait for him—even if his reasons are legit. Because if they're not, he's the only one who knows and you play the ninny.

In a single girl's quest to appear interested but not anxious, make sure you're not always the first to say hello; he's just as capable of noticing you logged on as you are of recognizing him (ditto for online meeting sites). Just because you can contact a guy doesn't mean you should. If your system's on all day and you're dyyyyyyying to send him a hello or confirm plans, don't. Nobody who causes you this much anxiety will keep you happy for the long-term. It won't kill you not to reply to an IM on random occasions, even if he sends one first; boost the mystery by being less available. Stare longingly at his avatar, if you must. He can't see you drool.

When you do hook him online, how long should you wait until you flash your sexy side? Well, if you've already met and developed a brassy connection, I suggest jumping right into hot and bothered mode—while making adjustments, according to his response. If you aren't able to deliver in real life, moderate your timing and tone. But know that sizzling text combined with an active imagination does wonders in the can't-wait-to-see-you-again department. "I'll admit that some women have gotten me semi-erect, just over IM," confides my friend Adam. Enough said.

🔔 don't be a baby in the bathwater!

Although techno-relating lends itself to fast-paced exchanges, it's imperative that you do everything in your girly might to suppress any hint of needy instincts if there's a lull in the conversation. Oh, admit that you have them. Lots of us do. And given how accustomed we've become to immediate gratification, techno-relating has conditioned otherwise calm women to become disproportionately clingy to how we act in person. I know, because I'm one of them.

When I first began using IM to flirt with a very slick cad, I couldn't have been more fidgety while waiting for his response upon hitting the Enter key. And because I didn't have to watch my partner's reaction, I'd swallow my pride and type something overtly obnoxious like: "Hel-LOOOO!!!" when he'd disappear for over three minutes. Once, he joked that my reaction to his absence startled him, and made him feel like a father who's left an unsupervised child in the bath for too long.

After this not-so-subtle jab, I began using the term "splish-splash" every time I felt ignored. Sure, this wasn't much different than my previous cry for attention—but written in lowercase letters, with a hint of self-deprecation and a reference to a joke *he* made first, my anxiety became palatable . . . and if the planets were favorably aligned, even endearing.

My point: Rapid-fire texts and IMs lend themselves to separation anxiety, and create an expectation of closeness that's difficult for a lot of men to maintain. The upshot is that if your boy likes to gab, your inexplicable hunger fools him into thinking you're simply sharp-minded and nimble-fingered when you're relating twenty seconds apart. Rather than provide you with a list of ways to pass the time while waiting for an IM or text reply, I want you to tweak your thinking about the male response. Instead of worrying whether he'll hate or relate to a little splish-splash, date the kind of man who welcomes regular dialogue. If he's talkative and witty in person, he's more apt to enjoy any type of communication—especially the incessant kind.

3. If It Looks and Beeps Like a . . . Text Message

When used to seduce, a text message can be just as powerful as a virtual wink: quick, coy, and strategic. But no matter how many characters your phone lets you to type, limit your note to two screens or 140 characters—or risk a partner's wandering eye. Given that cell phones are practically attached to our hands (or belts, in geekier cases), there's no reason you shouldn't return a text message within the hour—and at the very latest, twenty-four hours. If you opt for the latter, consider ringing the person to reply to their thought or question as a delinquent make-nice. And unlike with email, there's no way you or your recipient doesn't check your phone every few hours—whether at work, on a train, or getting off a plane. To delay a reply is to send a definitive "I'm ignoring you" prompt. Prep for repercussions, if you care.

So how do you balance the time-driven allotment of appearing too forward, anxious, or anonymous? It's a tricky precipice, I know, and it really depends on your personal MO with men. If you like to flirt extensively, establish games of tag at lightning-fast speed. If you can't wait for face-time, use digital chat to establish how and when to meet up. You've sent distant mass text messages to friends about Friday night plans, but what about using text to make more personal contact with someone you like? When delivering a warm text message, timing becomes secondary to intention. My neighbor Joanna lost her boyfriend in a bookstore, and blushed when her inbox beeped with the message: "Meet me in Romance." Text messages can provide near-intuitive access to soft, fleeting thoughts. They're the playful middle ground between talking and not communicating at all.

Other timing imperatives: It's a fine idea to send your guy a text an hour after your dessert date, but keep the message brief and personalize with an inside reference. ("Thanks for fun night. Sweet dreams, cupcake.") If you must abruptly bolt from a group outing to meet a friend in need, a quick apology via text the next day clears up confusion. In this case, immediate text would say he was on your mind all night; a call would appear too anxious; and ignoring the situation altogether is disrespectful. Catching on?

Although most send text messages as often as they converse, there is no right time to do so in front of another person—unless he's somehow involved in the message you're sending. Otherwise, three people are virtually in the room. Even if you're having an affair or planning an escape from a crap night, it's best to text from the bathroom. Just keep "Gotta pee!" trips to a three-bolt maximum or your guest may suspect a bladder infection or serious coke habit. Common courtesy should never disappear just because technology acts as an extra appendage. Try to be 100 percent present—and use the twenty-four-hour return-message window to give the other people you care about the attention they deserve.

Which reminds me: Don't underestimate the power of screening. No matter how much your guy hates it, screening is a must for harried girls who collect invites and reject the losers via txt msg. Why spend an hour on the phone fibbing your way out of a plan, when you can devote that energy to re-applying makeup for someone you want to be with? Now that's managing your time.

>>excuse you, brazen tongue. care to tone it down?

I dare say, a girl's urge to aggressively flirt and talk more openly via gadgets is a hard hankering to resist. I'm all for unleashing your inner bad girl (or silly girl, or genius girl) when you're reeling in a man, but please make sure the end not only justifies your means, but also parallels them. In other words, don't mislead a guy into thinking you're smarter, funnier, or more sexually forward than you are in real life—because at some point, you'll have to deliver. Think about it: If you paint a perfect yet unrealistic picture of yourself, then there's nowhere to go but down when you connect in person. If you portray yourself as a minx or mouse in the virtual world, you'll fail to find love in the real world if that's not the real you. Personally, I flirt much harder over technology because I enjoy the rush of knowing someone wants me as badly as I profess to want him. If I amp up my vibe, it's twice as exciting to anticipate a response. The problem is that when my techno-persona says harlot, and my in-person aura says demure, my date's virtual blue balls make him frustrated, annoyed, and confused. And that's not fair to anyone.

Best case scenario: If you suspect that he notices a disconnect in your online and off-line attitudes, demonstrate a happy medium so he thinks he has something to look forward to in the future. And in truth, he does! You obviously have it in you to follow through, or else you wouldn't have known what to say to begin with. It's okay to need more real-world time to warm up to your alter ego. When techno-relating, I suggest you work less hard at selling your personality and concentrate more intensely at communicating it. Manage your own expectations here too, because a guy's online charm and charisma rarely maps out perfectly in real life. Brace yourself for a mumbler who's funnier online, or a smooth talker who forgets to hold open your door. Techno-relating creates a false sense of immediacy during which you're convinced you've gotten to know someone very well. (*But his email was so deliciously biting. Why's he such a wuss in real life?*) Though sparks can fly when you techno-relate thanks to a well-crafted tone, remember that there's always a chance that he'll suck too hard on a toothpick and you'll bolt after one drink. Anticipate human error, even if you thought you experienced love at first type. Until a brilliant chemist is commissioned by Apple to transmit pheromones via computer (and I'm sure someone's working on it), the most exact voice-driven notes will never guarantee live chemistry.

>>advice for the tone-deaf

Nay-sayers argue that techno-relating will never measure up to phone conversations because tone can be easily misunderstood. But you know what? They're not 100 percent right. While it's easy to be irritated, surprised, amused, or turned on by someone's vocal inflections, a well-practiced techno-relater transfers her emotions onto a page or screen by making the most of language, punctuation, and emoticons. (If you can transfer an iTune playlist from your laptop to phone, shifting feelings from one medium to another will be cake.) Allow very little to get lost in translation, since the recipient will bring his own attitude and mood to the message when he reads (and rereads) your text. Since the way you talk is inextricably linked to your personal style, the best thing a guy can tell you is: "I can hear your voice when I read your words." Well, second only to: "Your words make you look really thin after eating an entire pizza." But you have a better shot at the first.

Spin through these tips on how to say what you feel, and note the example of each. Though some may seem obvious, feel free to modify the rules so they become your own.

✉ **All caps:** I know you're thinking "old news," but you'd be surprised by how many people don't know that ALL CAPS MEANS YOU'RE SHOUTING. OR MAYBE THEY DO—AND I'M THE OBJECT OF THEIR NEGATIVITY. HMM. IN ANY EVENT, DON'T DO THIS UNLESS YOU FEEL YOU'RE NOT BEING HEARD. FOR EXAMPLE, YOUR EX WANTS TO BORROW MONEY, OR YOUR JEALOUS DATE ACCUSES YOU OF

FLIRTING WITH HIS FRIENDS WHILE PLAYING POOL—
AND THEY'RE JUST NOT. GETTING. THE POINT. A good
rule of thumb? If you have to scream in all caps, you should
really be having this talk in person.

> *I don't care what it looks like in* People. *I was NOT
> CANOODLING with Jake Gyllenhaal!*

✉ **Asterisks:** Use these fancy little stars to preface a footnote
or ennunciate a single word or phrase as if you were using
italics. It's best to avoid using *real* italics, because a lot of
programs aren't able to translate the slanted letters. (Your
lovebird may wonder why you're sending him encrypted
code like a secret agent—and are you naked under that
Burberry trench?) Another good use for this symbol: When
you're in the mood to curse, substitute a letter with an * so
postmasters don't get huffy.

> *I'd *love* to meet your uptight parents for Sunday
> brunch, but I promised the girls we'd paint our toes pink and
> drink mimosas instead. I'm looking forward to a good
> bullsh*t session. . . .*

✉ **Contractions:** Shortening words with a cute little apostrophe
helps with colloquial writing. You'll also sound exceptionally
Type-A if you don't smoosh text together, just as you would
when talking. Be sure to always use the apostrophe, and for
the love of Strunk and White, stay away from the
"whose"/"who's" trap when making the most of those
'tractions.

You won't believe how quickly I've recovered from my Brazilian. Come and get it, babe. . . .

✉ **Dash:** Invoked strategically, the dash can be your BFF when emphasizing tone. End a sentence with a dash to imply a pause, or use the longer em-dash just before you make an important point. It's so versatile, you can also use a short dash to begin and end a letter (before/after a salutation).

You're right. I should not call you a psychopath, but I have a hunch that it's not normal for you to spell out the phrase "Drop dead" in dried rose petals—two years after we broke up.

✉ **Ellipsis:** An ellipsis is not an excuse to go dot-happy. Keep your periods to a sequential three to imply "um" or that you're trailing off with an incomplete thought. Drop a hint, follow it with an ellipsis, and let him fill in the blanks. Don't connect multiple sentences with an ellipsis instead of punctuating or dropping to another line. This creates a really long paragraph that reads as if you have CADD (Communication ADD—and yes, I just made that up).

I'm not wearing any underwear . . .

✉ **Exclamation points:** Assign yourself a quota of two exclamation points per message, max. If you must, save one for the end of your correspondence to add emphasis. If six out of seven of your sentences end with this overzealous punctuation mark, most guys will assume they don't have the energy to keep up with your cheery attitude. NEVER (yes, I'm screaming) use more than one in a row unless you want the reader to think you're on some really good crack. From a tone point of view, the reading voice (not to be confused with the crazy voice) in your head drops a few octaves when you drop exclamation points; you'll sound a bit more sophisticated when you talk, and dry-witted when you dig. Unless your intention is to sound overenthused about your bond (because we all know how well men respond to eager interest too soon in the game) . . .

I had such a great time last night. I've never seen the original King Kong, *but I'm so glad you made me watch it. Next time, I'll call shotgun on movie rentals. It's only fair. . . . Talk soon!*

⊠ **Extra letters:** Repeat letters to draw out a word, as if you were saying it in person. Most often, this is done when mocking the way someone else speaks. And don't worry: Nobody will assume you've made a typo if you repeat the letter more than two times. This rule is also applicable to expressing emotional reactions like oooh and aaah.

So daaaaaaaaaarling, are you honestly asking me to be your plus-one for the Marc Jacobs show?

⊠ **All lowercase:** You're so casual and lax that you've made the Shift button your bitch. Who needs it? Writing in all lowercase letters is more about style than tone—but you'll exude an overall laid-back attitude if you're consistent about writing big thoughts in small letters.

what time do you want to hang out tonight? i can meet you after yoga, around 7 if that's cool . . .

✉ **Parentheses:** Using parentheses is an ideal way to inject frustration, fear, humor, and sarcasm into a message—without actually including it in the main statement. Sure, it's a tad passive-aggressive. But parenthetical statements get your point across—and give you the out of pleading the case that your primary point is really your secondary one. Parentheses are also a great way to tease with a punctuation mark out of context. For example, if you speak in parentheses when talking dirty over IM, it reads like a forbidden (whisper).

Sure, I'm free to watch your garage band rehearse this weekend (and if I get a better offer, you'll be the first to know). I'll even feather my hair and wear a vintage Mötley Crüe T-shirt—just for you, my aspiring Tommy Lee.

✍ ha! what your laugh says about you

Very few things are more indicative of tone, style, and personality than a unique laugh. To hear a dear chuckle from across the room is to identify and revel in a familiar voice. Though emoticons and LOL deliver a genuine "I'm laughing! No really, I am!" message, I like to stick with phonetics that actually sound like the laughter that would ordinarily spill from my lips. Common giggles follow, along with an explanation of what each says about your persona. You funny girl, you.

Ha: You likely have creases under your eyes, thanks to squinting from concentration. Who has time to laugh? Yet add an exclamation point, and "Ha!" now doubles as a spontaneous guffaw.

Haha: You're a no-frills classic—a traditionalist, when it comes to self-expression. I'll bet you wear cashmere turtlenecks and drink Diet Coke with a straw, too.

Heh: Short, but definitely not sweet. Often interchangeable with Mwahahahaha.

Hehe: Easily embarrassed or silly by nature, hehe is a more broadly acceptable form of "teehee." If you woo with "teehee," you laugh at a supervisor's jokes with "hehe." "Hehe" says, "Notice me—but not too much." You enjoy acting cute, but always within boundaries.

Hmph: You're fed up and pissed off, with arms crossed for dramatic affect. Do I detect a pout?

Pft: Either cynical or dismissive, you're not easily amused. Your humor and tastes are discerning.

Teehee: With a French-manicured hand covering Nars-glossed lips, you're a flirty young thang. For more urban peeps: "Tee to the hee" sends the same vibe—if you're down with that shizzle.

Mwahahahaha: Sinister, much? Someone has a trick up her bell sleeve. . . .

>>is that an exclamation point in your pocket?

BY NOW, IT SHOULD BE PRETTY OBVIOUS THAT techno-relating is all about knowing how to finesse language and read between the lines. A little ESP wouldn't hurt either—but a sixth sense is hard to come by. In a way, maintaining a smart and fun relationship, both with and without a gizmo in hand, has a lot to do with well-intentioned manipulation. It's a matter of applying what you've learned in the past, marrying it with your own personality, following your gut intuition—and based on a joint connection, forecasting what might win his heart and warm yours in the future.

Before technology became such an important part of the dating game, the process was a bit like chess: We made lateral movements on a singular plane. But now that your guy contacts you on his phone that's also a camera, stereo system, and small robot all rolled into one—which may or may not be compatible with your phone, email, aromatherapy candle, and vibrator combo—the game involves more pieces than ever before. Forget chess, sister. You're playing chess meets Chinese checkers meets Chutes and Ladders—all on multiple planes, with many more pieces. Your boards have different boards. And if you're not tempted to engage because you're some kind of Anti-Tech Zen Master who's determined to float above the fray, then God bless. But know that this also means you're in the vast minority, and at the very least should know how to make text and language work to your advantage—even when you relate on the simplest levels. Because the way we talk online will slowly change how we connect in person.

In this chapter, we'll deal with the specificities that make or break a dialogue, and the language nuances encased in each. You already know the overarching importance of text, timing, and tone—as well as the effect that mishaps can have on your sugarplum's impression meter. When techno-relating, a slip of the finger is the equivalent of a tripping tongue. And if you don't nail the details, your guy might not nail you. Nobody wants that.

Aaah, the details. That's what techno-relating is really about. The way you sign-off an email, the allure of a double entendre, and the cheeky joy of misusing emoticons all play a role in your dating success rate. The same way a smutty note tucked into your guy's pocket once got him hot, your own DIY sex scandal left in his DV cam now has the power to turn him on and turn him loose— on you. Pamela who? That woman's work was amateur and low-res compared to the MPEG-4video and 5 MP stills that connect to his PC or Mac with a USB 2.0 and 128 MB card . . .

Yeah, I don't really know what the specificities of that last sentence mean either, except that they have the potential to help you land the guy you want. Submit to the power that's a Best Buy employee, and have strong faith in your minx appeal.

>>what's in a name?

Unless you're a celebrity or author with a nom de plume, most of us aren't wont to change our names so willy-nilly. Not in real life anyway. But when we techno-communicate, nicknames and email addresses and IM handles allow us to play with our monikers, which are immediately connected to and reflective of our identities. Even bloggers, who pride themselves on their ID, change names for anonymity and why-not sake. My advice? If you want to get creative, tag yourself carefully, because just like you, guys are quick to make judgments based on the text that's literally under their nose. There's only so much a person can go on, because we're denied the privilege of visually gauging a reaction to batting eyelids or charming words—and then adjusting an MO to carve out mutual rapport. This is why we start with a name.

When Mom and Dad chose yours at birth, they spent nine painstaking months pouring over paperbacks that talked about the ethnic, religious, or mythological derivatives of a title that would stick with you for life. If your parents were an indecisive lot, you were assigned "boy" or "girl" on your birth certificate for the sake of stamping you with some kind of identity (I actually know a guy whose parents went with the "boy" hold-over, but soon decided to name him John. When they made the legal changes, the word "boy" was never taken off his certificate—and he's been called John Boy ever since. But he's a theater actor, so it works). Jewish women are given Hebrew names when they're born, and Catholics are baptized with holy names they share with saints. When you were young, your name was probably shortened for the sake of adolescent cachet—but even nicknames had to pass muster with your own sensibilities (You might have only changed back to your full name after your first job interview). I remember the popular girls always had built-in nicknames—made more enviable if brevity whispered androgyny, like Mel or Nik. And if Hallmark magnets and key chains didn't identify you, it's almost as if you didn't exist at all. No wonder the world embraced the rhyming genius of Shirley Ellis, who made everyone feel special with "The Name Game" song in 1965. Without a recognized, desirable name . . . you might as well be invisible.

With such history buried in our pretty subconscious, it's no wonder we place so much emphasis on the consequent identities we assign ourselves. I mean, it's easy to blame parents for a shitty legal name—but like a big city, the Internet is a breeding ground for self-reinvention. And the starting point for that is the text you use to identify yourself. Unlike in conversation, when we look at a screen, we see the name as well as read it in our head—which means it has twice the impact. In some cases, letters are visual statements as much as they are practical ones used to form a complete word; in others, they're meant to be heard differently than they read. I think the easiest way to approach naming text is to stop talking about it and start showing you what I mean.

>>pseu-pseu-pseudonyms

I know a relationship columnist named Esther, who argues that when choosing a pseudonym for yourself, address or handle, a dramatic name change says you're not comfortable with who you are—which then leads to the assumption that you have a constant need to please other people. "When you create a new name, you have to be careful because the person who reads it doesn't have the context of you as a whole person," she says. "Potential dates will just react to a word on a screen." That said, when choosing a name, be sure to think about how it couples with the attitude, intelligence, and overall image you're putting out there.

On dating and community sites, choosing a suitable name tells the world how you want to be seen. Consider your intentions: What kind of people do you want to attract? What do you want their first impression to be? A name like "Twiglet" or "KitKat" sends a playful message, while "BigOldNastyHo" sends quite another one. "AreolaRavioli2" tells boob men you're at your best in cold rooms, or "Kristinainpajamas" implies that you work at home (or don't work at all). If you're corresponding with a guy named "Playdough," you may end up in Vegas for the night; and if you're angling for a commitment, "Marrymetomorrow" might just be your soul mate.

Without a doubt, all names ironic, idiosyncratic, or wordplay-related score points across the board. My friend Alia, a photographer from LA, calls herself "cAliafornia" on IM—which immediately says she's witty and proud to be a West Coaster. Choose a pseudonym like "Sublime," and the porn-star moniker insists you're a Double-D catch. But if you're not careful, misunderstandings can rear their no-man-clature heads: Esther, the relationship columnist, says that when she online dated, her faux name was "Queen Esther"; too bad this invited a slew of transsexuals who took the title "queen" too literally. . . .

Of course, there are always names that defy traditional English spellings and/or resemble license plates. They capitalize in strange spots, drop out vowels, and basically botch our forefathers' language. "ForBiddeN" is one of the most popular friends on MySpace—and nobody cares that her name shits on convention. In fact, it makes men want her more. Know, however, that askew grammar skews young (and often, simple-minded), so your biggest fans will follow suit. For the most part, mature communicators either use their real names or creatively play with their initials. Plus, these are the most easily remembered should one's address book crash.

When assigning yourself more than one email or IM address, be sure to brand yourself with appropriate verbiage for personal and professional use. Unless you're a Midwestern bombshell who also happens to own a profitable fruit farm, peachfuzz@allsmiles.com might send the wrong message to clients.

>>salutations! salutations!

Like the fabled spider Charlotte, you're sending messages via the Web—except your salutations speak to an audience beyond snorting pigs and singing goats (hopefully). Let's break down the do's and don'ts of how to address a short- or long-term interest d'amour. My friend Stephen insists that salutations are closely analyzed by guys, and he personally considers them the "canary in the coal mine" to gauging a relationship's status. He claims that men are always looking for signs that you're interested—and here's where they start reading into you. Stephen and his friends suggest that when saying hello and good-bye, you should be emotionally exact with your words.

Evidently, there's nothing worse than hearing that you sign messages with a word like "kisses" to him—as well as peers, friends, wine club members, and the Amazon.com rep. Like every suggestion in this book, you might find that as you become closer to your guy, your relationship demands that you punch up your text to reflect your compatibility. When this happens, you'll have already established a strong enough link that you won't need too much advice, because you'll have cemented your own techno-relating groove that can't be replicated. That's probably one of the most wonderfully intimate outcomes of our seemingly impersonal mediums: Once you've built techno-synergy, you've developed a language that belongs only to you and yours. Like a kiss or touch, this can be incredibly personal.

Who You Callin' Dear?

No matter what stage of a relationship you're in, save the formalities (Dear, Hello, Mr.) for thank-you notes and performance evaluations—unless you're being glib. If you're sending an email, start the string with a greeting, but go casual with variations on the word "Hi," and always use the person's first name unless it's the kind that usually has a built-in nickname. Names like Marcus, Robert, Jonathan, Joshua, and Bradley are likely shortened on everything but credit card statements. However, you can't be too sure until he signs off first; follow his lead for future notes. Addressing him only by the first letter of his name is a sly move, too. Lead up to silly monikers like "S-Dott" for Scott or "G-Star" for Greg, so you don't sound like a party promoter, A&E exec, or famous rapper—unless you are, in which case authenticity takes priority. After three consecutive email strings, drop the salutation altogether. By now, you're having a conversation.

And my dearest Pookie, watch those terms of endearment. "Babe," "Hot Stuff," and similarly lax names are well-received. "Doll" and "Sweet Pea" are also safe after you've had sex. But venture into Love Muffin land, and he's bound to freeze up (or barf, whichever comes first).

Hugs and Kisses? Already?

Knowing how to sign-off can be a tough call, since you don't want to be too affectionate, but you should never be so dismissive as to ignore a farewell altogether. Overly formal good-byes are as much a no-no here as overly formal addresses, so steer clear of "Good-bye," "Sincerely," "Yours truly," "Best regards," or "Best." Brief and darling words like: "Yours," "Bye," and "Mwa" are a perfect balance between friend and more. Avoid "Talk later" or "Talk soon" unless you have definitive plans to do one or the other. An ambiguous sign-off does not a warm impression make. Strangely however, "Soon" is assumptive in a forward and sexy way. (*See you soon? Go out soon? Make-out soon? Tell me more...*) And please, avoid "Take care" at all costs. It's the ultimate kiss-off, best saved for the final ditch.

I know this will come as a surprise, but nine out of ten men

I spoke to found the popular "x," "xox," or "xx" sign-off to be a really misleading, aggressive, or audacious good-bye. In fact, one guy relayed that the letters remind him of his grandmother's holiday cards! Considering most men don't know that "x" means kisses and "o" means hugs, they'd just as soon back away from affectionate maneuvers before you've declared a serious relationship. Your best bet? Save the tic-tac-toe symbols for girlfriends, even if you're a natural-born flirt. The same rule applies to typing "love" or "luv." Although most women assume that "luv" is the friendlier version of "love," the same way that "love ya" is the less-intimidating version of "I love you," men don't want to analyze the minutia. Again, if you're in a relationship then all bets are off. But until he says these words in person, I'd avoid jotting them out on a screen.

The only time I've seen the love/luv/xo/x sign-offs work to everyone's praise are when they're either combined with or used in lieu of your name. Your name plus emotion, squeezed into one symbol, is like a tattoo or wax seal. It's a symbol of your identity—and I've never met a guy who didn't dig it. For example, my friend Johnny signs off with "xJ," as his friend Amanda shortens her name to "xa*" (I'm told the * represents a twinkle in her eye). I even know a woman named Beth who combines sentiment with her first initial to create "lovb." With men and women, I always end a note with a punctuated "xx" or simply "x"—which I imagine is the equivalent of an air kiss on both cheeks ("xx.") or a quick kiss ("x"). I seldom use my name or its initials—and nobody's ever questioned who the note is from, or assumed I was mauling them with smooches (coupling with lowercase notes helps). Using symbols instead of names, minus endearments, emanates a sense of visual hip. Chloe, an Internet designer, signs all emails "+c" and her friend Katie uses "kt"—which is both visual and auditory. Just avoid overly interpretive symbols. You are not, nor do you ever want to be, the editor formerly known as Emily.

If you're more of a traditionalist, simply sign your name as you would on any other correspondence—depending on the degree of intimacy you have with the recipient. A first initial says casual, but avoid using the initials of your full name, which is better saved for professional messages. Monogrammed letters, in which you switch your last and middle initials, as if embroidered on towels or sheets, is always out. No need to mention your name when finishing a text or IM message, either. It's redundant. And as I mentioned above, three or more email strings qualify as a conversation, so lose the sign-off here, too.

should you give multitaskers the flush?

Consider the classic riddle: If you download a song onto your camera while emailing a coworker and Googling an old flame, but nobody's there to see you, did it really happen? And more important, does it make you a vulgar sod?

Well, it depends. I say there's no harm in multitasking if your third party doesn't know he's only getting half your attention (i.e. if you're not in his presence). Realize, though, that your baby shouldn't detect a multitask using any of his senses. There's little worse than pouring your heart out on the phone and hearing your mate tap on his keyboard. It's kind of like using the phone as you pee: If you don't have permission, it's an overt insult—and a hard habit to break.

>>when the medium's the message

When techno-relating, what we consider to be language extends beyond the use of our conventional alphabet. The ABCs of conversation also include visual and auditory elements, which means making custom podcasts, using emoticons, connecting with web cams, and sending images from your phone are just some examples of how we expand the definition of text-based chats. And when that's the case, your medium becomes an important part of the message. Since you're now attaching sound and visuals to words, this instantly brings you closer because more of your senses are involved in the communication.

Sure, you can send a "Happy B-day!" text from your phone. But isn't a camera phone shot of the words scrawled across your exposed stomach, in harlot red lipstick, much more enticing? And logging onto IM when you're on the road keeps you connected, but a video chat from a hotel room is much more private. Using strategic tech to bring you closer to the physical person is how channels do their best to bond, not alienate, two people. And when timing, text, and tone work together, I can't think of better foreplay to a next date or postmortem to a previous one than sending a let's-get-interactive message. In every case, the mediums and messages are linked.

But before you let those creative juices flow, follow a few guidelines when pushing boundaries. Like reciting a poem or accepting a bouquet of flowers, delivery is everything. The fab news is that each time your guy receives a message, you reset the bar for the type of techno-relationship you want. Which means his turn to please you is just around the corner.

If you want to nix the singing telegrams, then it's time to surprise him with tech-driven treats to tell him he's on your mind.
When sending a message, take the following into consideration:

✉ **DO get personal:** Play off inside jokes and references made
during live or online dialogue. Knowing that any creative
overture via tech will seem like a major effort because the
juxtaposition is unconventional, a private allusion says
you're listening—not stalking.

✉ **DO keep it quick and dirty:** Technology is about expediency,
and though it might take you a while to create his surprise,
your guy's reaction should be immediate. You want him to feel
like you effortlessly understand each other. An instinctive smile
is your goal.

✉ **DO be low-key:** If he has to click, download, and print for
hours, think again. You want to say you care, but not so much
that you sacrificed a whole weekend for his five-second
smirk.

✉ **DO make him want more:** Like any well-crafted
message, your gift should solicit a response. Think of it as
an email that ends in a question. Ideally, he'll reply with
a similar gesture, thank you in person, or use it as a
catalyst for establishing the individual groove we talked
about earlier.

⊠ **DON'T go overboard:** An hour-by-hour montage of your weekend sent via email will not only crash his system, but kill his interest. With each token, ask yourself: *Why would he want this?*

⊠ **DON'T regift:** If a gesture worked with another dude, don't recycle it in the name of previous success. Two times isn't a charm; it's unoriginal. What if he forwards, prints, or posts it on his blog or webpage? This isn't a good way for him to meet an ex for the first time.

⊠ **DON'T solicit a response:** He'll love your treat, guaranteed. But if you don't hear from him for three solid days, avoid sending a note to the effect of: "Did you like it? Did you? Did you?" If he doesn't react to your gesture, your crush is either an ingrate, uninterested, or both. Forget him.

⊠ **DON'T extend yourself too often:** The way he gushes about your thoughtfulness is not an invite to up the ante with hourly, daily, or even weekly gestures. You held out your hand, now let him kiss your palm. He needs to show his appreciation and prove his value, too.

Just remember: New mediums are designed to enhance relationships, not to be used as a crutch to avoid real contact. If abused, techno-relating can prolong an initial date or add more space between encounters. Frequent tech communication is no substitute for a cozy meal at home or day-long hike through the mountains. If your relationship feels like it's moving too slowly, the medium is no longer your friend. Rather, someone's making a very loud and clear announcement about one's inability to step up to the next phase of the relationship. Don't allow (yes, allow) gadget-gabbing to get in the way of building in-person bonds. You control technology; it doesn't control you.

✒ isn't it romantic?

Sending techno-gifts requires a little creativity and a whole lot of confidence. After all, you may be making the first unconventional move, which can be admittedly scary. The amazing news is that if done correctly, your guy may view you in a brilliant new light. Any cute girl with nimble fingers can craft an alluring profile or message. But after a few exchanges, only you know how to make his toes tingle by giving a good gift. Keep in mind that new tech will always overlap, usurp, and overwhelm the old—but even if you're not strapped with the latest and greatest, you're still posing on solid ground. Just remember to be as image-driven as possible, since men are innately visual creatures, and follow the "If it looks like an email and formats like an email . . ." theory to follow trends with minimal performance anxiety. A few ideas to begin the brainstorm:

✉ **Bring Back the Mix Tape:** Buy him a Playlist, or make one of your own. When a sexy girl crossed the quad in college, my roommate used to joke: "Man, I'll bet she has lots of mix tapes." Count on your guy to return the gesture. You'll be That Girl in no time. . . .

✉ **Is That My Teddy?:** Great for long-distance relationships or meet-me-in-Miami jaunts. Shoot a favorite item he loves (think: snack, stuffed animal, or personal item from home) in multiple locations when you're en route to see him. Send pics via phone, so he'll have a record of its kooky journey. This way, he'll also be able to track how long before you two connect in person.

✉ **Phone-in-a-box:** Buy-one-get-one-free phone deals are so rampant these days that you'd be silly not to send one to your sweetie. Messenger him a neatly wrapped box tied with a bow, and stash a phone inside. Ask the delivery guy to call you just before he drops the package, so the box rings as your guy opens it. You'll be on the other end with a throaty hello and shared calling plan!

✉ **Tease His Appetite:** Gearing up for the holidays? Sending vaguely cropped jpegs of real presents you plan to give sparks curiosity and excitement. It also reminds him of how much you deserve in return. Space these out over time to build anticipation or all at once as a fun collage. You can also send a similar tease leading up to a date or anniversary, with images of what the big night might entail. A bra strap here, the corner of a restaurant sign there . . .

✉ **Text a Treasure Hunt:** Send your honey on a hunt, with clues sent via text message. After he finds each gem, have him send you a quick note—"yes"—so you can drop the next clue. Idea: The final item should be you . . . holding an invitation, carrying a real present, or wearing nothing at all.

>>for a good time, im (your handle here)*

Phone sex is so ten years ago. And I don't care how strong your cell's vibrate function is, no wireless device can service you the way IM sex can. If you must, use your phone to play music as you articulate just what you'd like the emoticon with a wagging tongue to do to your thigh.

The best thing about IM sex is your ability to reinvent the significance of emoticons—and build sexy anticipation until you rendezvous in person. I know Skype and Google Talk let you speak *and* IM with partners, but there's something to be said for kicking it old-school with AIM (AOL IM) or iChat when you're having screen sex. And while there are hundreds of downloadable faces on the Internet, and even "hidden" emoticons from Yahoo that IM fans can tap, I suggest sticking with the standard sixteen you receive upon registration. If you want to get kinky with puking, monkey, and devil faces, I sure won't stop you. But I've always thought that the best off-line sex marries basic technique with lots of imagination; similarly, extra frills have no place here.

When I read about live sex, I find it insulting to be given specific, Twister-like instructions on where my hand should land—while my head goes here, and my foot fits there. How-to sex guides read too much like an IKEA manual, and IM sex is not about mass-produced faux wood. When it comes to a good romp, men appreciate a customized knowledge of sweet spots, and an innate ability to massage them. It's this carnal instinct that you'll use during IM sex, as you

*If you're an IM sex virgin, don't worry if your first time's a bit clumsy. You'll get better with practice. If you're a natural, save yourself for men who deserve the open-mouth emoticon—and limit your partners to two at most. If you don't control your libido, you'll risk a slutty online reputation. The last thing you need is to find your IM handle scrawled on a personal webpage (the equivalent of a bathroom wall at the Viper Room).

laugh and purr your way to a good time. Just don't forget to fly a generic "I'm away from my computer now" flag to avoid interruptions (it's the IM equivalent of a tie on the doorknob).

Read through the following wicked possibilities of what each IM face could mean, though you'll control the specifics of your experience. If ever there were a time to type dirty, this is it. So mute that computer and turn-up the Barry White. You've got some inserting to do.

☺ : innocent smile; happy with his/your suggestion

☺ : surprise; blow job; the start of an orgasm

☺ : big spender; pay for sex; strip club ref

☺ : confusion; regret; disappointment

☺ : rejection; guilt; bloated from too much dessert

☺ : kisses; cover you in lipstick; let's include a transvestite

☺ : foot fetish; drunk; feeling tired and stupid

☺ : sad it's over; together, two of these could mean blue balls

☺ : on your side; if you know what I mean; a teasing agreement

☺ : angry; yelling; piss me off and you won't get a blow job

😫 embarrassed; scolded; caught with your pants down

😷 bondage; let's keep this a secret

😋 : panting; playful; oral sex; licking in general

😎 : overblown ego; obnoxious cool; you'd rather be at the beach

😇 : use after a tawdry thought; idea: let's use a diaphragm (or protection, in general)

😁 : the end of a major orgasm (best preceded by three open-mouth faces)

📖 was it good for you?

After hot dates, my friend Erin and I play a game in which we see if we can describe the night *only* using emoticons. Words and sounds are an option if the bald heads slow down the description or cause confusion (For example, emoticons don't 69 very well; consequently, the long narrative reads like R-rated Mad Libs). Though it's easy to excuse the yellow faces as cheesy, using them in a crude exercise promises lots of laughs. Give it a try! They're hieroglyphics for the horny.

>>cyber sleuths versus cyber sluts

When perfecting the art of techno-relating, it's essential to look for online and off-line cues about how to move forward, when to pull back, and when to go in for the kill—without being an animalistic tramp. Before you instinctively reply to an email, have IM sex, or send him a Web cam image, make sure your guy's sent you the right message first. I fully condone being the aggressor, but only when your partner signals that he wants to be aggressed. I'm not asking you to repress your sexual wiles, but I do think that techno-relating elevates extremities in a person's attitude—from shy to seductive. And I wouldn't want a guy to misunderstand your intentions, especially if he's a keeper. So like Inspector Gadgette, be sure to follow clues that will cement you in his memory. Pace yourself intuitively; this is what separates cyber sleuths from cyber sluts.

Because everyone's techno-relating style is different, your goal is to avoid projecting your feelings onto his persona. It's easy to assume you're on the same page when your libido, frustrations, or anxieties fill in the blanks between four lines of tag. Just beware of mishaps! And follow these text-based tips out of limbo land—if, and only if, you combine them with inside refs, conversational writing, and a realistic sense of yourself (bonus points for a sense of humor).

✉ **If He:** Writes diatribes about life, flirts like he's in love, but never asks you on a date
Then You: Choose four words from his missives that could be easily misconstrued if out of context. Your only response is one sentence: "I'm sorry, but you just used the words 'hot,' 'pursuing,' and 'strapped' in that last email and I'm still recovering. . . . Is there something you wanted to ask me?"

Why It Works: You've stirred his hormones, implied yours are on autopilot—and asked him a direct question that tells him you're interested, pronto. His head and pelvis should be in the right place for an invite. If his response evades the question, don't bother to reply again. He's more interested in a pen pal than a girlfriend.

✉ **If He:** Cancels a date, but types that he'll "make it up to you . . ."
Then You: Ask him how, in so many words. Speak in hyperbole here, so he's amused but not intimidated by your forwardness. "I'm so glad you said that, because I've always wanted to go diving for pearls or play craps in Monte Carlo. Is that what you had in mind?"
Why It Works: He knows you're still interested, despite his crap move. Over the top suggestions make it easy for him to take it down a notch, as in: "Monte Carlo's pretty far away. But what about a night at the Indian casinos, upstate?"

✉ **If He:** Spends an hour flirting over text, when you could be on a date . . .
Then You: Elevate the flirtation to such heights that he's about to burst in anticipation of a response—and then stop sending texts altogether.
Why It Works: He'll be so turned on and confused about why you didn't reply that he'll call. When he asks why you didn't respond, tell him: "Why waste money on text messages when we could spend it sharing a bottle of wine by the river?" He'll drink you up before you finish the vino.

✉ **If He:** Waits until the day-of to ask you out via email or text . . .

Then You: Accept, but only if he gives good reason ("I had a lame day, and the only thing that'll cheer me up is sharing a sloppy burrito with you") *and* if you've had three successful, planned dates already, which makes this a whim. If he pulls the move before you've been on great date #3, tell him you have [specific and enviable] plans with a "friend." And then make some.

Why It Works: Techno-relating lends itself to casual, last-minute invites because of its casual, fast talk and delivery. You can be relaxed without being too easy-access. Set a standard about dating preferences before your fourth date, or he may fall into a lazy routine.

✉ **If He:** Has seen you naked at least six times . . .

Then You: Send him faceless Web cam images of yourself, clean or otherwise.

Why It Works: He'll love the visual message, but it can feel forward during the initial stages of a relationship. If he's seen you naked more than six times, that means 1) you're both less vulnerable to each other, in general; and 2) he came back for more, even after you squeezed his love handles and he laughed at your "Peas on Earth" T-shirt and panty set.

✉ **If He:** Has made it to second base at least twice . . .

Then You: Can initiate IM sex.

Why It Works: IM sex is perfect foreplay to perfect foreplay. You'll establish likes and dislikes in a mischievous venue—

any of which you'll laugh about in the bedroom. Ignite sparks with suggestive references, and set the tone about what kind of lova you are (silly, sexy, teasing, etc.). PS: Just because you've had IM sex doesn't mean that you should feel obligated to deliver in real life. But I imagine you already know that. Make sure he does too.

✉ **If He:** Ebbs and flows, emotionally—depending on the day, his mood, your fishnets . . .

Then You: Try writing with double entendres, until he steps up. Grammar and punctuation jokes are playful, considering your medium. For example: "I don't usually type this fast before a third date. . . ." Or if you're feeling extra racy, "I don't like to keep a man's participle dangling . . ."

Why It Works: You don't know if he's playing push/pull games to heighten the tension, or if his interest is waxing and waning. Here, your best bet is to follow his lead—but move according to your own specific rules. Play the humor card to take the edge off. Saucy double entendres will either drive him over the edge or encourage you to take those semicolons elsewhere.

04:

>>type the talk

WHEN TECHNO-RELATING WITH YOUR HUNK DU jour, you're interacting in a world that's both familiar and intangible at the same time. And as I've said before, using technology as a main vehicle for communication tends to warp time, escalate expectations, and create a sense of assumed intimacy. This means that as the evolution of your relationship soars at an unfamiliar pace, so does the process of learning about your guy. Consequently, how you understand your connection will inevitably affect your self-image, sexual excitement, and in general, who you are and how you handle living in a world of constant interruptions and compulsive energy. The last thing you want is for your budding rapport to be clunky, misunderstood, unnatural, awkward, or uncomfortable. When it comes to dating and technology, the words "go with the flow" have become altogether archaic. Either that, or the flow's morphed into a rush.

Though I could easily wax poetic on this topic, I'd rather mix things up with expert opinions for credibility's sake. "Couples send technology-driven messages out into the world without a lot of forethought," says sex therapist Patti Britton, PhD and president of the American Association of Sexuality Educators, Counselors, and Therapists (AASECT). "We've developed this manic finger behavior that's very commonly a knee-jerk reaction to a feeling or mood someone's sent our way." It's so true, isn't it?

When we don't balance cyber and live interactions, Dr. Britton asserts that one-dimensional communication devices dehumanize the initial dating process. So even if you're essentially having more human contact with more people via technology, it's a very thin slice of the real thing. She warns against expecting too much, too fast—and adds that just because you're connecting multiple times a day with a crush doesn't mean your interactions are meaningful. "Techno-relating can throw a relationship into overdrive before you're even in first gear," she says. "It takes time to know somebody and develop a relationship beyond quips and flirtations on a screen." Consequently, Dr. Britton says we need to be incredibly self-aware about how we feel every step of the way—because it's easy to substitute real knowledge about a person with an "idealized fantasy."

So how should you acknowledge these tricky psychological elements—yet still build interest while maintaining sanity? As you know, the ability to connect with (and even better, arouse) a person over technology is incredibly powerful, especially since so much is left to the imagination. Yet knowing how to make this work for, and not against, your intentions is what will separate you from the competition and keep you off your analyst's couch.

There's something to be said for romantic anticipation when baiting and snagging a mate—and in case you haven't realized it yet, techno-relating is an exercise in extremes. If it doesn't speed the courtship process, then it forces us to slow down. There's no middle ground, no sense of controlled pacing. I can't stress enough that the most reliable way to understand the quality of your coupling—every step of the way—is to use online communication to reinforce, not define, your relationship. This minimizes trust issues and tone misperceptions: major stumbling blocks when noting the difference between a progressing relationship and dots on a matrix. An alphanumeric keypad isn't going to make your relationship, but it could break it if you're not careful. Ultimately, you want a substantial bond. But you won't reap the benefits of patience, love, trust, and empathy in the real world, if you don't know how to define these in relation to cyber boundaries.

>>baby, you can trust me

Techno-relating takes trust issues to a whole new level, especially since it's impossible to determine the dynamics of relationships beyond your own when you and your guy obviously connect with people outside your happy duo. How can you trust that your lover won't forward a note to his friends and neighbors? How can you trust that he's not flirting with other women without scrolling down his text message inbox to invade his privacy? How can you trust that the dirty photos you took last night on his digital camera won't be posted on his blog the next day? The new means by which trust issues have expanded throw insecurities, violations, validations, intrusions, and various levels of perceived risk into overdrive. It can make a girl nuts.

Remember the bright side: New modes of technology add a new dimension to your relationship, so that even on the busiest days or at the most inconvenient times, you can check in and say hi. You can receive a one-liner that says "You're beautiful" and then smile through a grim five p.m. meeting. The sweetest text I've ever sent was at a packed, loud party in which my boyfriend was on one side of the room, and I was on the other. I couldn't see him through the sea of black, so I sent him a note: "Missing you, even if we are in the same room." Two minutes later, his hand was on my shoulder. In this type of situation, techno-relating adds an extra level of intimacy because you're secretly communicating in the company of others—without subjecting strangers to your mush. It's the equivalent of exchanging glances across a crowded room; only this time, you're reaching out with discrete words and not shmoopy facial expressions.

Of course when you share info over a phone or computer, you do place your faith on an unstable precipice. We've all seen the nasty fallout of trust gone sour when personal sex tapes are posted on the Internet or scorned exes forward break-up emails as revenge. And when it comes to cheating, skimming a cell phone bill can be as tempting as digging through a man's pocket for an unaccounted-for jewelry receipt. Even call and text message logs can be the demise of a relationship. My friend Charlie's roommate, who we'll call Smarmy Bastard, learned this lesson all too well. He and his regular sex buddy, who also had a boyfriend, often exchanged a simple "Come over" message via text when either was in the mood. Cut to a random Saturday afternoon, when SB answered his mating call—and received a serious beat-down by the girl's boyfriend. Evidently, the smarter BF hacked his girl's text log and sent the repeat message to confirm his suspicions that she was unfaithful. SB escaped with limbs intact—though his dignity was shot to hell.

We could easily extract that the obvious lesson here is "don't cheat." But more to the point, if you don't want something read, don't write it—or in SB's friend's case, delete it immediately. This not only goes for text messages, but for notes sent over work IM or email. If you treat every message you receive with the assumption that it will be read by strangers with a bucket of popcorn, your edits not only decrease reasons to doubt your trust in another, but also help you establish communication boundaries without actually saying them. Even if you're saying less, your sense of intimacy will inevitably increase because you'll become comfortable with your digital dialogue. And once you establish a comfort zone, trust and respect will follow. By nature, we believe in people who exhibit honest qualities—and the Internet lends itself to brutally honest disclosure because of the anonymity factor. So if your guy's a good one, his sincerity will only help support the trust you two are working to establish.

Once you've done this, questionable trust caveats of techno-relating, like cutting and pasting emails of a friend's advice, won't feel like sneaky or insincere moves. If you think about it, poaching a girlfriend's wisdom is no different from—and actually an extension of—asking her opinion over Sunday brunch, and then reciting her words as if they're your own in a tense situation.

Ideally, all communication would only be kept between you and your partner, but techno-relating doesn't lend itself to that pact. Yet once you establish boundaries, the trust issue becomes more about your relationship and less about the communication mode. Distrust of any kind, cheating or otherwise, really comes back to the people in the relationship: If you're one to engage in shady practices, you'll always find a way to sneak around. The "T" word always circles back to a person's character; blaming the ease and frequency of new mediums is too simple.

In other words: The simplicity with which you build trust in your relationship parallels your demonstrated convictions in the cyber world. According to relationship therapist Joy Davidson, PhD, who also hosts the online video series The Joy Spot about human sexuality, reliability doesn't become more precarious because we have new and more abundant ways of breaching it. "In any relationship, there's trust or limited trust or boundaries of trust—and all of that comes from the same experiences in one's life and relationships as it did in the old days before technology was a prevalent communication medium," she says. Multiple messaging options serve to validate our trust in someone or provide opportunities to show they're untrustworthy. If anything, Dr. Davidson feels we're better off now than we were before these mediums existed. "A person's character has more ways to shine through in the manner in which they use technology," she says. And the way a person uses technology (his behavior) says just as much about him as the message (or words) he's sending.

Dr. Davidson, however, does forewarn against abusing the ease and immediacy with which we trust another person as we build tech-driven relationships. "Having multiple options can mean using them in lieu of genuinely connecting," she reminds. "There's a misunderstanding that if we send five emails, we've connected, but we've just exchanged information in isolation. Don't mistake techno-connection for genuine connection." Toss the illusion that you've spent more time with this man than you have. According to Dr. Davidson, there's a tendency among women to imbue a partner with more faith this way than if you were to have spent just as much time with him, minus techno-intervention. So while it's true that emailing and text messaging can help you know someone better, it doesn't mean you've known them longer—or have been able to learn anything about them that they aren't willing to share on-screen. "Real trust is developed over real time, based on behavior," she insists. "It's about how it comes through for you in actual practice and what you intuit about a person in actual behavior." Trust is not wishful thinking, but based in action and self-confidence, that coveted POV which refuses to let an outside force knock your soul off balance. The amount of heartfelt belief you have in each cyber relationship is proportionate to how much trust you invest in yourself.

✍ how to bust a cyber cyrano

Come clean, sister: You have at least one go-to friend who has written (or edited) some form of techno-communication sent to a man you've tried to impress. Or maybe you've played Cyrano yourself. But have you ever wondered if you were on the receiving end of a cut 'n' paste moment? And would you even know if you received a Cyranote?

Personally, I don't see anything wrong with helping a distressed girlfriend cobble together a message. Women love to help friends in need, and if all it takes is using an innate skill to combine thoughts and feelings into a perfect sentence, so be it! Women borrow from one another all the time when we step onto the advice pedestal like Dr. Laura or loan a roommate a cherished Dolce & Gabbana dress for a formal date. Men know this, and they even expect it from our sex. We innately like to analyze, share, facilitate, nurture, and communicate. Playing Cyber Cyrano is just another way that we fulfill each of these small needs.

However! If you suspect that your guy's recruited his own personal Cyrano, I suggest you bust him sooner rather than later. Don't call me a hypocrite; there's method to my madness. Unlike women who most often rely on friends of the same sex, men most often turn to female friends or confidantes for relationship advice. This is fine when it involves storytelling that relies on recollection, but I personally prefer that other women lack the intimate details of my words—especially when they're about an impending, slippery, or rocky romance. I'd rather read a man's sloppy or overtly direct verbiage, because then I know the kind of guy and behavior with which I'm dealing. And as a woman, you know damn well that if you were the author of a Cyranote, you wouldn't be able to walk away from the drama that makes for voyeuristic gossip fodder. You'd want follow-up, involvement, and the freedom to read the woman's response to your well-crafted message. Already your darling's Cyrano knows far too much about your relationship, and how his mind works . . . especially in tandem with hers. It's one thing to have a partner in crime, but something else when she's operating behind your back. Not to mention: Women are a sneaky lot when it comes to romance, and if they have their own agendas, men can be obtuse to their wily ways. You know what I'm talking about.

Sound neurotic? Maybe a smidge—but I like to err on the side of caution. Better to call him out now, than three months down the line when you've dropped the L-bomb and he thinks he's in the clear to articulate on his own. Well, look at that! Now you're suddenly disappointed because his notes aren't up to par. Nobody likes a poseur, even if he only feigns linguistic skills. In any event, memorize these clues to better detect whether your partner has another partner.

- ✉ **Change in font details:** Is there an inconsistency in quote marks, apostrophes, or characters?

- ✉ **Unusual spacing that indicates a forward:** Please say he was smart enough to remove the >

- ✉ **Change in capitalization style:** Does he vary caps and lowercases, as if he cut and pasted? Or did he once write in all lowercase, and now he emails with grammatically correct cap skills?

- ✉ **Differences in spelling and grammar:** Is he better or worse? Don't simply credit spell-check . . .

- ✉ **Change in email length:** Does he elaborate more often? Become introspective? Speak metaphorically?

- ✉ **Change in thought exposition.** Is he more or less verbose? Does he write in "I feel" statements?

- ✉ **Variations in phrasing and word choice:** Do you recognize unfamiliar slang, for example?

- ✉ **Amended punctuation:** Does he use dashes, where he once used periods? Does he write in short paragraphs, though he once favored run-on sentences?

- ✉ **Variations in tone:** Has he gone from flirtatious to formal? Is he less sarcastic than usual?

>>imagination, anticipation, and communication

When your guy's IM window or email address pops onto your screen, it's not unusual for your imagination to take off and running. Whether that means picturing him at his keyboard in boxer briefs, multitasking in a three-piece suit, or reading your mind because he just knew you'd understand his two-word text message, fantastic scenarios can't help but run amuck in your head. Which is good news, because it means you can creatively squeeze 3-D potential from a flat, word-based medium—so long as you don't project your feelings onto vague situations and personalities that are more enigmas than engagers. Obviously, the less you know about a guy, the more you can imagine that he's more like you. The biggest problem with this is that if he isn't forthcoming, then you're forced to fill in the blanks with what you want to see. Dr. Davidson, our trusty shrink, says that it's when techno-relating lends itself to outright fantasy that you've entered murky waters in real life. "You can lose a sense of reality when you're with someone after you've idealized them in your head," she reminds. "The difference can be jarring. What doesn't come through in technology are stupid jokes, bad posture, and horrible breath— all the stuff that's hidden in a neat email but overt in face-to-face contact." But as Dr. Britton, our other trusty shrink, notes, techno-relating allows your mind's eye to see someone from the inside out—which is a rarity at any stage of dating. "Instead of looking at a guy's mirror image," she says, "technology gives you the advantage of getting to know someone by how they communicate. Communication is the key to all healthy relationships."

Although techno-relating demands you trade real ideas, your brilliant imagination still appreciates the relative anonymity of cyberspace and allows you to access a side of yourself that's playful or more forthright than usual. And if you can deliver consistency in person, Dr. Britton suggests you go for broke "as long as you're not fundamentally lying." She says that honesty about age, weight, and marital status are the biggies—though I'd add details about family, friends, and criminal records to that list. "Your imagination isn't usually activated when you meet or spend time with someone traditionally," she says. "But techno-relating strips us of our superficialities and the need to meet idealized standards of beauty."

Now that you're determining compatibility based on like-minded typos rather than passable taste in boxer briefs, also assess similarities and differences in your emotional state when you're communicating online and off. If at any point you feel like you're connecting with two different personalities (his written and real-life personas), confront your loverboy in person before calling an exorcist. Feeling broken, disappointed, or criticized when you meet in the real world also demands that you resort to regular dating protocol and dump the twit after serious consideration. Your off-line emotional state is a lot more important than your online one—especially if being together makes you feel lonelier than when you are by yourself.

>>what's on your mind?

Part of the reason anticipation adds so much to techno-relating is that gadget talk speaks directly to the male brain: It's clear and unexpected. A one-line email toward the end of a hard workday, or even a text when you know he's left a meeting, will transport his mind out of the office and into a private space. I'd never put words in your mouth, but even a simple "Caviar tonight. Served on my stomach?" is plenty to supersede a guy's frustration during his hellish commute.

The underlying surprise-message tactic is nothing new, but it's always proven effective. Remember when your mom tucked love notes into your father's briefcase before work? Me neither, but I hear that happy duos in their generation did. Your turn involves sending electronic sentiments that he'll carry in his messenger bag.

Some argue that while reading words on a page or screen makes a man's brain operate, it doesn't provoke the same sensory images as a voice on the phone because you're still one-dimensional. These are the men who demand the most bang for their BlackBerry buck—and also forget that talking on the phone with a woman can be time-consuming and awkward, especially if she's nervous.

The flip side to romantic anticipation is, of course, the needy factor that technology tends to cause. I know we touched on this earlier, and I know you're not clingy in real life. But the fact that instant communication can unleash paranoia is a topic I'd like to revisit for a teeny sec since we're discussing the role of romantic anticipation and imagination in dating. When techno-relating, there's a fine line between regular contact and pestering—and the major difference is in your delivery, his receptiveness, and your collective timing. Because so many men are attached to their gadgets, and yet often lack dating confidence, they need your cues to express interest.

When one friend expects a date to be in touch, he says his mind goes something like this: "What do you have a cell for, if you don't answer it? Why are you online, if you can't talk to me? Why are you logged onto IM, if you plan to ignore me all afternoon?" Sure, this proves that men can be just as nervous about slipping past your radar; but it also reinforces that men expect women to be in touch with more frequency than we might expect. The easiest way to feel confident about playing tag and making regular contact is to match mediums. After all, you're angling for an equal partnership, right? For example: If he calls you, then you call back; if he emails you, then you email back. If he texts, and you call, that's great too—but only because it's a communication upgrade. As long as your return is of equal value or you're moving up the hierarchy, then you won't be stamped as disinterested or passive-aggressive (with the exception of screening, which isn't appreciated, but is a necessary evil for a girl in demand). Just make sure that the amount of time you spend techno-relating is proportionate to mutually expressed interest.

>>defining your limits

Creating online boundaries for yourself can be a daunting task, mainly because you want to stick out your exposed neck—but you don't want it to be Photoshopped to a donkey on a bestiality website. So how do you take risks to define your limits, without feeling violated if wires cross between you and your mate?

Because your relationship exists in the real world too, Dr. Davidson recommends you ask yourself these two questions before making a precarious move: "If I existed in a tech-free universe, would I act similarly?" and "Would I do this if it weren't so easy?" What trips so many of us up when creating limits and crossing lines is the speed and simplicity with which we can act. We hit the Send button, and hope for the best. So the next time you're tempted to email a topless photo of yourself, think about whether you'd feel okay handing it to him in person as a gauge. Consider these common scenarios to help you delineate your own boundaries.

✉ **If You Wouldn't:** Introduce him to your three best friends . . .
Then Don't: Include him on a mass email to your entire clique.

✉ **If You Wouldn't:** Confess your heart-thumping love to him in person . . .
Then Don't: Use any of its written derivatives in a sign-off like xox or luv.

✉ **If You Wouldn't:** Tell him basic stats and demographic info about your exes . . .

Then Don't: Post their pictures on a community site and call them "friends."

☒ **If You Wouldn't:** Discuss your dreams of 2.5 kids and a picket fence over tapas . . .
Then Don't: Send him shots of nieces, cousins, or your friend's kids via camera phone.

☒ **If You Wouldn't:** Whisper your favorite sex move in his ear at a party . . .
Then Don't: Spell it out over email, you closet floozy.

☒ **If You Wouldn't:** Confess your unrelenting obsession with Luke Perry . . .
Then Don't: Tell him you have a blog, especially since Luke's face is its wallpaper.

☒ **If You Wouldn't:** Play striptease in the bedroom . . .
Then Don't: Send him a choreographed dance over your Web cam.

☒ **If You Wouldn't:** Invite him to dinner with your parents . . .
Then Don't: Involve him in a three-way call with your grandchild-obsessed mother.

☒ **If You Wouldn't:** Accept a year's worth of blooms from the Flower of the Month club . . .
Then Don't: Send him a link to Tiffany.com.

✎ um, your cursor's in my personal space . . .

Techno-relating lends itself to an open-door policy that's made intrusive communication a norm. While info overload affects fewer people than tech virgins might expect, establish where you each draw the line anyway. "Just because your bum is there, you don't have to show it," Dr. Davidson says. "Similarly, just because we have technology at our fingertips, you don't have to use it." Fair enough (and nicely put), though most daters I know embrace new ways to grow and change with advancements—albeit, at their own speed. Hanging back reminds me of people who held out on buying cell phones because they didn't want to always be accessible. Now, these same techno-phobes wave their neon Nokia screens at Billy Joel concerts in place of lighters.

More appropriately, I'd discourage using more than four forms of techno-relating at a time, even if your man's a techno-junkie. Just be sure to tell him if you pull the plug on one medium; explain yourself so he doesn't falsely internalize why he's been cut off. Showing him how you feel with a delayed response (or none at all) simply looks like you've lost interest. To avoid sounding like your mother ten years ago, I suggest making your case a time- or convenience-based argument. "So sorry, but crazy sched lately. Can we stick to email and phone?" sounds a lot better than, "I feel most comfortable only talking via email and phone. What do you prefer? I certainly don't want to be intrusive." Although you're essentially saying the same thing.

"We're talking about physical space in cyberspace," says Dr. Davidson. "In real life, there's a certain degree of physical space that feels proper and comfortable. If someone violates that, you step back to maintain the boundary. With these technologies, you're examining targeted dynamics which bypass that sense of testing physical space. The only way to tell if someone's comfortable with these new mediums is to ask."

>>modern is not to be confused with sociopathic

SCARY, BUT TRUE NEWS FLASH: THERE'S A SUBSTANTIAL number of living, breathing humans out there who use technology as a substitute for living, breathing interaction—and you don't want to get involved with any of them. PhDs like to call their tendencies sociopathic, but I fear that's a bit strong and clinical for our purposes. So let's roll with the term socio-pathetic here, though the similarities between the two are quite obvious.

In brief: Socio-pathetic men hate leaving the house, assume multiple dating personas, and/or lack basic functional social skills. They entice you to step into their life—despite the fact that they haven't showered, shaved, or eaten anything but Cheez Whiz sandwiches for a week. These men will chase you, flatter you, and yet never encourage live interaction because they're nervous, reclusive trolls. They have trouble discerning between right and wrong, and the only persona a socio-pathetic dater puts out into the world is a false portrayal of himself.

For obvious reasons, this is not the kind of man you want to take home to Mom (or your cat, for that matter). And yet, when we start to feel increasingly intimate with someone thanks to hours spent online instead of time spent in person, you can see how one might slide into this trap. Please don't be the enabler of a hermit. As one fan of substituting online interaction with live encounters tells me (let's just say he's been known to flirt, send gifts, and techno-relate for up to four months . . . without ever meeting): "I can control the way I communicate via technology, and if I can control one medium of communication, why pursue another where I feel less confident?" What he doesn't realize, and you now do, is that as more time passes between encounters, the more active your imagination becomes—and the greater your chances of feeling let down when you do connect in person. Although a socio-pathetic personality thinks he's saving himself from rejection, he's actually increasing his chances of it.

If you and your mate exchange sentiments over tech, but seldom indulge face time, I suggest you strongly evaluate the relationship's future. Your guy shouldn't use gizmos to hold you at a distance, hide information, or question your intentions either. We're all afraid of the emotional reveal, but when a mate cowers behind a portable laptop or phone that barely covers his face, the situation is frustrating at best. You don't want to be with a man who hides behind a lit screen and well-crafted sentence, someone who spends more time impressing you over IM than over an antipasto for two. And you don't want to be the woman who condones hours of IM tag when you could spend that time on your sofa watching *When Harry Met Sally* . . . with someone worthwhile—hopefully, lip-locked during the really talky scenes.

After all, the best part of techno-relating is connecting the dots between a person and his persona. You're above reclusive dating tactics, whether you're happy or grumpy. Which reminds me: Don't let the socio-pathetic ball bounce into your court. When talking through important issues, for example, it's easier to zap off a nasty note than to initiate an in-person dialogue. But is it healthy? Carefully notice when an online spat is about to cross the line from constructive communication to passive-aggressive tantrum—and stress that you're a modern chick in search of a sane relationship at that time. When you strike the balance between raw and real, you'll present yourself as the right woman for the right man . . . in exactly the relationship you want. And let me just tell you: None of this involves a recluse or processed cheddar spread.

☜ is he shy or socio-pathetic?

Your love bug texts you into the wee hours of the night. He makes you laugh over email, as if he were a hetero David Sedaris. After an hour of IM sex, you're left breathless and craving a cig.

But what if his real-life banter doesn't measure up to his online shtick? Or he cancels every third date, but tries to win you back with an animated monkey e-card? You tell yourself he's just not an extrovert, and he reassures you he needs more time to feel comfortable. Excuses, excuses? The line between shy and socio-pathetic is fuzzier than the dice that hang from his bedpost—and you only know they exist because he shot them for you with his video phone.

The following list differentiates between an acceptably reserved man and one who plays aloof one minute, interested the next, and downright cagey in between. If four or more of the below point to an all-too-familiar socio-pathetic personality, I suggest you recommend group therapy and back away slowly. It's not your job to pry a crazy out of his apartment and onto your sofa. Save your strength! You'll need it to fend off hoards of well-adjusted men in your future.

✉ **Shy**: He emails you a shot of his face concealed by shadows.
Socio-Pathetic: He emails you a shot of Patrick Dempsey's face concealed by shadows.

✉ **Shy**: He sends you a text to ask if you're fighting.
Socio-Pathetic: He sends five angry texts, but ignores your calls between each.

✉ **Shy**: He's too bashful to spoon, so his feet snuggle yours.
Socio-Pathetic: He asks you to sleep with your Web cam, so he can sense your presence.

✉ **Shy**: He dazzles you with quick wit over IM, but struggles in person.
Socio-Pathetic: He dazzles you with quick wit over IM, and repeats each joke in person.

✉ **Shy**: He avoids introducing you to his family.
Socio-Pathetic: He avoids introducing you to his family, though he lives in their basement.

✉ **Shy**: You meet his friends one at a time.
Socio-Pathetic: You meet his online friends, one at a time—until you realize they're all him.

✉ **Shy**: He pauses before telling you he's from an interfaith background.
Socio-Pathetic: He stalks both Christians and Jews.

>>you're SUCH a *$#@!?!

Like any good argument, kicking and screaming over cyber-space is satisfying at times—and little more than a headache at others. While it might be easiest to spit venom over a wireless handheld and face the repercussions later (or skip town and not confront them at all), this doesn't necessarily mean it's the best way to duke out frustration. Take a deep breath while I explain.

When considering whether to strike the keyboard or your boyfriend's face during a kerfuffle, first assess your anger level as well as the issue's potential to tumbleweed into a bigger brawl. If even the smallest part of your intuition suspects that a misin-terpreted tone, delayed reply, or abbreviated response will make either of you smash your laptop into small pieces, it's best to fight your battle in person. Only you know how sensitive you are, how prickly he is, and how well you're both able to seamlessly share and interpret the other's feelings. If this is your first fight, try to think of a similar situation that provoked a strong reaction—and follow an analogous path back to bliss. This way, you'll have a backup rationale for your conscious.

If you decide on a cyber brawl, I suggest you spat over email (and if he doesn't check it frequently, send him a text message to do so). Using email as a format to discuss problems or share con-cerns is extremely useful because you can vent, reread, edit, and send the message phrased in a way that you hope will get your point across without sounding mean or cruel—and it might actu-ally be helpful to your relationship. In fact, experts say that this is preferable to blowing off steam in someone's face or blasting them on the phone. Over email, you have the opportunity to edit your words; the medium includes an inherent second chance. On a bigger scale, email gives you the forum to write a proper letter, which taps into a timeless art and tradition. Channel Abigail Adams for inspiration—she and John based much of their relationship on exchanging letters over two hundred years ago. Imagine how feverish their love could've been if they'd had Gmail accounts!

If you're on the receiving end of a fight and your guy vents and hits Send right away, his behavior is telling. Off-line, he's likely the type who explodes in person without a filter cap. You can learn a lot about a guy (or yourself, for that matter) by how he responds to your frustrations: with language, with brevity, with humor, or with heart. Ranting is a free-for-all, and if a person does what comes naturally, you'll see who the other person is, naturally. Like any other form of techno-relating, the behavior behind the message is an important litmus test for compatibility. The frequency with which we write, rant, criticize, and joke via tech is one big metaphor for how we project our identity and sense of self.

Don't be discouraged if you send him the most perfectly written, psychologically correct, agonizingly beautiful message, and it's badly received or misinterpreted in haste. Once you deliver the argument, the message is out of your hands and into his queue for analyzing pleasure. Techno-arguments are a gamble, since their interpretations rely on moods, schedules, and menstrual cycles. Some experts insist it's best to type, "We need to talk" and suggest a time to face reality in person. It's easy to demonize your beau if he's not seated in front of you.

Before you behave rashly, write a note that says you need to get something off your chest—and then wait to send it. This gives you time to cool off, walk away from the message, and reread it an hour later after you've sucked in fresh air, eaten a banana to raise your blood sugar, and decided that you may or may not feel the same way. Remember that when you send a feisty message, you're not screaming at a machine. Your recipient is a live, emotional person that reacts in the moment just as strongly as you might. Yet because it's admittedly tough to communicate well in a tense situation, techno-relating does allow you the control and distance you may need to voice your thoughts. Just don't neglect follow-up interaction. To properly bitch online, focus on engaging discussion as opposed to blurting your feelings in a one-way dialogue. Even if this argument blows over, you and your guy will piss each other off eventually; you might as well work out the kinks on how to have a constructive back-and-forth now.

Realize, however, that with the start of a fight comes the obligation to finish the conversation. Unlike an in-person encounter, techno-relating gives you the option of spewing a message and then mentally shutting down. If you sign off during a tense moment on IM, realize that it's the online equivalent of slamming the phone or storming out of a room. The phrase, "RckstrLova has just signed off" can punch harder than a fist. If you're frustrated enough to pick a fight, then you need to be responsible enough to listen to your partner's reply.

And just like an in-person argument, the worst thing you can do is pull the silent treatment. An online argument is not a one-way "Screw you" with the sadistic plus of watching him squirm with future "Did you get my note?" follow-ups. Believe it or not, the most difficult part of having an online spat isn't so much in delivering the message but in waiting for a response and interpreting its honesty without body language cues. You can't watch a man's face turn red, hands fidget, or sweat-beads gather at his hairline (assuming he has one). Visuals can even indicate whether he's really sorry or simply wants you to shut up. But if you're arguing online, a delayed response on his part or yours might be misunderstood as the silent treatment, when the truth is that he's been called into a meeting or you're taking time to write a thoughtful reply.

Just make sure that you're griping online for the right reasons (smart dialogue, self-restraint) and not the wrong ones (an easy way out if you fear confrontation). In a trusting relationship, the happy medium is to send your guy a note, let him stew over your text, and then discuss your frustrations in person. By the time you meet up, you'll both have digested the info and mulled over talking points. So when should you take your kid gloves off-line? Trust your gut. If you need to broach a serious conversation about, say, the tramp you suspect he paws behind your back, you'll know that tech mediums are inappropriate. Also, if you're not getting each other's point or his answers aren't fully satisfying, consider meeting in a neutral territory outside your home. This is a great time to gauge body language too.

Arguing in person requires a certain amount of courage, but a real-life conversation means you'll have the chance to hold hands or look into each other's eyes. You can also adjust your approach if you notice a tear or slumped shoulders that you wouldn't consider in separate rooms. Even the simple act of saying "I'm sorry" is more genuine in person. You'll understand feelings behind statements that are a lot harder to assess in an instantaneous digital format. Plus, when you argue in person, you cut conversation time in half since you have more to go on than words. Which also means you'll have more time for make-up sex.

when you just need to "agh!"

He pissed you off. You bit back. And now that you've both waged a full-out e-war, all you want to do is let out a cathartic scream before you ask him to finish the talk in person because it's become an unreasonable swap. You could curse at the monitor as your coworkers bear witness, but I prefer using an initial huff in the Subject head of an email to communicate succinct exasperation without making the main body of my message too emotional. Don't stretch out the letters of a yell or groan, because drama is not something to which men respond well. But a quick outburst drives the aggravated point home. Changing the Subject with each exchange works nicely too. If you begin by saying "Last night," progress to "Are you KIDDING me?" and end with "Argh!" Your escalating emotional state is the first thing he sees in his inbox. Nixing salutations by cutting right to his name or even its first letter adds particular emphasis. Like this:

```
To: Bensucksass@guiltybastard.com
From: Aperfectangel@wink.com
Subject: Ugh.
Ben—
Your last email doesn't even warrant a response.
We need to talk in person. Free after 7 tonight?
K
```

Easy, right? These Subjects also say you're about to lose it—but
saving the Big Spill for him:

```
Subject: Aaah!

Subject: Argh.

Subject: Hmph.

Subject: (None)

Subject: Patience: Testing 1, 2 . . .

Subject: UGH!

Subject: What a joke.

Subject: WTF?

Subject: %*$@#!
```

>>clever? (check!) sincere? (check!) irresistible? (check! check! check!)

So far, I've endorsed honesty, colloquial speech, and more than a
little sass when communicating your character and intentions.
Much of this relies on having the self-assurance to say who you

are and what you want—with unrelenting exactitude. This means no lies, no cloaked vocab, and rare occasions in which you withhold the truth. (For example: Trickle-in family secrets as your comfort zone increases; he doesn't need to know that Uncle Earl's fourth wife invented the smokeless ashtray right away.) Bluntness is actually easier than censoring your words to an extreme because your style is a direct reflection of who you are as a person. And when you're strolling along the river with his friends instead of chatting online among a friends network, you want to be as open and honest as you can, because that's the person who's most attractive to another. Easier said than done, of course, especially if your job or lifestyle has made you into a deliberate wordsmith—and if your sense of precision, at this point, is subconscious.

I can't untangle your psyche, but I can tell you that when you're too exact with your language, you risk hiding your spontaneous or silly side, which probably turns more heads than you realize. Writers, lawyers, and educators are among the top professional types that use words to specify intent on a daily basis. When techno-relating, you need to stop putting on face and hiding behind business speak. You're not drafting a memo or sending an official email to your boss in search of praise. You're relating with an affectionate person, someone who uses your words as a means to understand your intentions and gauge your personality. Like it or not, you are what you type. And if you type like an uptight bitch, well . . . you fill in the blank.

My advice? The next time you techno-relate with your guy du jour, lose the phone voice and text propriety—and run down the following checklist to make sure you're putting your best self forward. Draft that message, and then whip out the Montblanc pen to tick off the items you've accomplished below. Oh, admit it: Nobody rocks a to-do list quite like you do.

✉ dating to-do . . .

⊠ Swallow the impulse to use jargon like "As per . . ." or "With regard to . . ."

⊠ Lose time/date reminders about when you last connected. Even the phrase "After our lunch last Thursday . . ." is too formal and just specific enough to suggest you put a heart around the date in your daily planner. Don't let him think you care that much.

⊠ Replace general references with specific nuances when referring to your last date. "Dinner was good fun" is not nearly as original as "The way you slurped your spaghetti put the mutts in *Lady and the Tramp* to shame—in an endearing way, of course."

⊠ If you must sign off with initials, precede them with a sweet "Soon" or "Yours."

⊠ Don't enumerate ideas or opinions. He'll want to put a bullet point through your head.

>>hacked, busted, and back for more

I'M A FAN OF FULL DISCLOSURE IN A RELATIONSHIP— but this doesn't include doling out passwords or techno-relating details with men who could possibly threaten my welfare. There's only so much you should share with your baby, no matter how close you are.

Hoarding tech info is about privacy, and every relationship needs it. Give your guy the keys to your place, his own drawer, even a shelf in the bathroom, but keep all passwords to yourself. This has little to do with trust, and everything to do with maintaining your own sense of technical independence and freedom. You know that if he so much as glanced at one of your notes, the chances of him confusing a joke or reference is all too possible. Just like the telephone game you played as a kid, he's going to get your girlfriend gossip all wrong. That is, if he's not horrified by how much personal info you share with your friends first.

Knowing when your chest hurts from PMS or how funny you find his orgasm face does not a stronger bond make. . . .

In my opinion, giving up specific tech-details about your private life is an element of control a man shouldn't have over you, no matter how hard he tries to convince you that sharing will bring you closer. Tell him to save it for Dr. Phil, because real trust allows you to have conversations that don't concern him— conversations that he trusts won't let him down.

Of course, privacy isn't a one-way deal. If you don't give your guy the password to your computer, email, BlackBerry, dating accounts, community sites, or even your cell phone, then you shouldn't expect to be given his. This also means you shouldn't sneak onto his computer without his permission. What if you misunderstand what you find and it causes you a week's worth of angst? You're not Brittany Murphy in *Little Black Book*.

Take your guy out of the scenario for a minute, because it's really your happiness that I care about most. Now consider: Even if you found the most shocking info online, you'd struggle with whether to confront him or keep it a secret. You'd have to confess the situation to at least six friends for advice, and then they'd downgrade him from "lucky find" to "ungrateful yuck" without all the facts in tow. You'd be sick for days. The anxiety would eat you alive, until you were forced to blurt out that you are fully aware that his desktop has naked photos of his ex—and what kind of fool did he take you for? Oh wait, that was his roommate's computer? Oops. Shared trust issues would become a disaster, even if you worked on newfound insecurities. And if your guy never assumed you snooped in his drawers and bags when he wasn't around, he will now. What's worse is that he may now feel entitled to do the same to you. Talk about a vicious cycle. I have a stomachache just thinking about it.

Is this the kind of relationship you want to be in? I think not.

Now if you *stumble* across upsetting information, that's another story. Once, I used my ex-boyfriend's computer to check email, and when I typed in the URL, a scroll-down list of recently visited websites appeared for my convenience. Hello, helpful cookie function. All I needed to see was the word "x-treme" followed by the name Nathalie, and the cliché "How often do you look at porn?" fight ensued. I called him a massive perv and accused him of lacking "masturbatory imagination" (I swear, I did). I yelled, he stammered, and before we knew it, he confessed to past offenses I'd rather assume didn't exist. Cut to two days later, when my baby called to say he clicked on the URL I'd seen (but never visited)—and it was an extreme sports site he once used for work-related research! I laughed, but the poor dear had already busted himself; I didn't even have to be sneaky. The positive outcome? A genuine talk about the roles we expected tech to play in our relationship, and a vow never to intentionally invade or judge another's private matters without calm discussion first.

I'm not endorsing an "ignorance is bliss" lifestyle here. I'm suggesting that you value your guy as you expect to be valued yourself. If you have nothing to hide, you have no reason for doubts—and neither does he. Should your one-and-only pressure or even threaten you about this topic, no matter how sweetly he couches the subject, your self-protective instincts should shoot off fireworks. This man's interests are not your own, and whether they stem from insecurity or control or trust issues isn't your problem. A like-minded partner is exactly that: one who shares your principles. And if you give in about this topic, there's a good chance he'll only up the ante later. Today's password could be tomorrow's credit card statements.

calling all female hackers: you know who you are

Girls, girls, girls! I can't believe how many of you have snuck into your guy's computer, stolen his password, or explored his bookmarks like the Pink Panther hopped up on estrogen supplements. What happened to your "Do unto others" mantra? What happened to your faith in mankind? Oh, and what happened to the secret mistress your guy was keeping in Key West . . . ?

That's right. As much as I think busting into a guy's private world is very, very bad, the number of stories I've heard about how women's fears were confirmed when they did so almost legitimizes the means to their (relationship's) end. Even still, I'll never support this invasion of privacy, mostly because I'd be mad pissed if someone turned the scenario around on me.

So where does that leave you? Listening to your gut, and then verbally confronting your guy with any suspicious activity. You don't need to do the dirty work of actually proving his infidelity, gambling habits, or porn addiction. If your instincts say he's up to no good, if your friends think his behavior is fishy, then take him to task. Your trust issues will have trust issues if you keep it to yourself—and if his sensible explanations still make you squirm, nothing stops you from trading him in for someone with whom you feel immediately comfortable.

That said, I can't resist sharing a few tales from women who've read their guy's notes and wish to dish. Some had their worst worries confirmed, while others sought revenge or a good laugh. But even in the best-case scenarios, snoopy situations lead to increased vulnerability—which left their relationships on shaky ground. You didn't sign up for a panic attack, with a side of crushed expectations and low self-esteem. Why go there at all?

My college boyfriend and I dated for six years, and we shared a cell phone to save money. He dumped me for another woman and then married her five months later. Although he changed women, he wasn't smart enough to change phones. On his honeymoon, I broke into his voice mail and erased all the messages from people who congratulated him on his wedding! —Amy, 24

I dated a guy for two months who was intent on getting my password. He'd use every excuse in the book just to open my laptop and learn it. He wanted to IMDB actors we'd watch in a movie, he'd insist on running a search on an animal we saw on TV. It was almost comical, because I knew what he was doing. One day, he was at my apartment while I was working—and I noticed that my IM was logged on from another location! I called him, and asked if he was using it. He denied that he'd broken into my computer but it was obvious. I couldn't trust him after. —Jess, 33

My boyfriend left his phone on the bar when he went to use the bathroom. It was just sitting there: open, unlocked, ripe for the hacking. So I quickly scrolled through his text message inbox and outbox, but found nothing incriminating to speak

of. I felt awful after, but because it was there and we're together, I almost felt entitled to do it! I have complete faith in him now, but I'm sorry I had to be deceitful to discover this
—Kara, 26

Once I dated a guy who was introduced to me by a friend. Six months into our relationship, he confessed that in his past life, he lassoed dates via Nerve.com. So I dropped $30 on their membership fee and created an online fake profile to find out if his account was still active—and if he was still looking. My false persona contacted him, and immediately slid his favorite movie, book, and music references into a fictional girl's profile (sans photo). I basically created his dream date: a model that loves hard-boiled noir fiction and knows the Scorsese oeuvre like the back of her twenty-two-year-old hand. It's not hacking, but it was a major invasion of his privacy.

I'm fairly certain that by the time he read to the end of my fake profile, he came to his senses and realized that no barely legal model/actress would love Pete Dexter novels and the exploding palm trees from the opening scene of Apocalypse Now *as much as he did. Someone was fucking with him, and most likely that someone was me.*

I never got a response from him, and we never talked about the profile. When I went back to check on his response three hours later, I got the stock reply: 'We're sorry but that person is no longer a part of the Nerve.com community.' His online anonymity ended right there—and I dumped him a week later because all of these other random guys replied to the phony girl's ad. When I confessed that I'd just turned thirty and never wanted to be an actress, I actually dated one of the men for a few months.
—Veronica, 33

Two years ago, my ex asked me to go into his personal email and forward him an article for work. He was on the trading floor, and I was still at his apartment. After I sent it, I glanced at his inbox and saw a note with the subject: "Re: Hello Diamond." I saw the word 'diamond' and thought he might propose! So I opened the email—and instead, I learned that Diamond was a prostitute who he planned to fly to New York on my credit card. I printed one hundred copies and called my father, an attorney. He came over immediately—and told me he and my mom happened to hire a PI after they first met him because they didn't trust his stories.

The PI soon told me that this creep lied about graduating from college (he never went) and boarding school (he was in juvi!). He was married before, with kids—and he left me with $1500 in outstanding gym bills, which we used to threaten him with a fraud suit. The guy even said he was on a soap opera, but never was. The lies went on and on. He was a total sociopath with three email addresses and a rep for having sex with hookers he met on Craigslist. The PI said he'd email them within minutes of when I'd walk out the door to work . . .

Since my unhappy accident, I tell others that if they have the slightest suspicion that something's not right, they should immediately confront it. This man was a good liar, but that didn't muffle my instincts. I chose to ignore them. I'm a very private person now, but even still, I wouldn't endorse others reading private emails. I ran across Diamond, and I was lucky I did. —Laura, 29

Lesson learned? Keep passwords to yourself, and tell him from the start that you'll respect his privacy if he'll do the same for yours. Promise each other that you'll do your best not to give each other reason to doubt fidelity or sanity. And then mean it.

>>it's all fun and games . . . until it happens to you

Whether you're in a new relationship or dating around, you have every reason to keep passwords quiet. If you're still in the are we/aren't we dating stage, you may even be seeing other people—and if one happens to access an account, you can expect gallons of havoc to ensue. Truth is, nobody has the right to your private dialogues. Even if you feel close to a debonair newcomer, try not to gain a comfort level too quickly, and know you have better things to whisper in each other's ear than passwords and pin numbers. Now would be a great time to recall the psychiatrists' thoughts on arrested intimacy. There's a limit to how well you know the men who weave in and out of your life, so protect yourself first. One guy's family might run an Internet security system company and the other's college roommate could be an underground hacker. How would you know otherwise?

To help you play it safe, follow the tips below to make sure your privacy remains your own*:

⊠ Change all major passwords every two months; write them in a hidden spot if you're forgetful.

⊠ Make sure your passwords don't overlap from one medium to another. Numbering each one ("tennischamp1"; "tennis-champ2" . . .) is a tactic that hackers know all too well.

*Sound like a lot of upkeep? It's less than it seems—especially since your confidentiality is at stake. Until your routine is on mental autopilot, set an alarm on your phone or calendar to make changes and deletions at the end of each day.

⊠ Delete private items in your email save box and trash at the end of each day.

⊠ Delete your inbox and outbox text messages at the end of each day.

⊠ Avoid obvious passwords that relate to pet names, hobbies, years, or your lifestyle in general. Instead, use quirky habits like how you take your tea—two lumps of sugar, then stir three times might translate to: "2lumpsthree." The chances of someone guessing this are pretty slim.

⊠ Replace letters with numbers, even if you're spelling out a word. For example, if you choose to use the words "motorcycle mama" for your password, spell it like this: "m0t0rcyc13 m@m@."

>>it always feels like somebody's watching me. . . .

Until a scorned ex, persistent one-night stand, or suspiciously alert boss pokes his creepy nose into your business, it's hard to imagine that hacking can happen to you. Too bad Todd Snapp, the president of RocketReady, says it's easier than you think. Snapp's company provides "ethical hacking services related to social engineering"— which is industry talk for legal hacking that busts con artists. These scamps take advantage of people, as opposed to using computers to do the dirty work (human hacking, as it were.) Snapp also provides security services for corporations who watchdog employees over tech. So if you're wondering if HR could can you for snickering about your supervisor's shoe size or if your new squeeze has already memorized your credit report, read on.

Since social engineering is how most skanks have their way with your info, Snapp warns against this type of hacking first and foremost. Especially since you don't need a programming degree from an astute university to manipulate people.

Remember when Paris Hilton's Sidekick was hacked? That was social engineering at its finest, although most *US Weekly* readers assumed it was done via computer. With SE, invasive cons infiltrate their victims by pretending they're someone they're not. It's a cinch to call T-Mobile and act as if they're a customer who wants to reset a password, and with the right info (address, phone number, social security number), access their account. A smooth voice and a naive help-desk employee can be a destructive mix. Similarly, Snapp says to be selective about who you allow to use your computer. Slimeballs can email a help-desk from your computer or email. Some even create alternate email addresses that look like they belong to their victim (For instance, a hacker can create a Yahoo! account for you, even if you only opened a Gmail account for yourself). This way, social engineers have legit info for a false identity.

Shove computer break-ins to the back of your mind for a moment. Hacking–meets–identity fraud issues should bug you out the most. Because while you're busy putting up firewalls and assembling virus protection programs, social engineers are using non-tech methods to gain access to technical details. Snapp's best corporate clients employ him to break into their systems using human means to learn if he can gain the same access that a computer hacker would. He then chronicles his research in a document called a "vulnerability assessment." If Snapp were to compile a doc about your online lifestyle, what would your vulnerability assessment say?

For those who fear psycho stalkers (which is, like, everyone), techno-relating has both intensified live stalking and created a new type of cyber stalking. And no, I'm not talking about the way you track how long it takes your crush to IM when you're both clearly logged on, or how you notice on community sites when an ex immediately IDs himself as "single" the day after you've been dumped. Thanks to the Internet, it's easy to tap archived info as far back as ten years. That's helpful for researchers and reporters but grim news for stalk-worthy singletons. "I know so many people who've had to change their email addresses and IM names because a guy they talked to a year ago on a message board tracks them down everywhere they go," Snapp says. And just when you thought Google was only good for blind date back stories, Google hacking sparks voyeuristic impulses in a whole new way. Snapp says that using various codes, domains, file types, and email addresses, subpages of information are available to the pros. Which yields his final warning: Be careful about any conversations, blog entries, profiles, or photos posted on the Internet—because you don't want them to fall into the wrong hands. And never, ever reveal your social security number, no matter what your man promises in return. Hacking is like the grown-up version of a stranger inviting you into his Buick for candy. You didn't bite when you were a kid, so don't start now. Say no, and keep walking.

> ### ✉ gone phishing
> Your word of the day? Phishing. Using social engineering tech-
> niques, phishing is obviously illegal, but best characterized by
> a person's attempts to fraudulently acquire sensitive info like
> passwords and credit card details. Hackers masquerade as a
> trusted person or business in an apparently official electronic
> communication like email or instant message. The term
> comes from the use of increasingly sophisticated lures to "fish"
> for users' financial info and passwords—not from the hippie
> cult band with a stoner following. Although victims might feel
> like they're in a psychedelic nightmare. . . .

>>cautious or cockeyed? the truth about hyper-vigilance

Believe me, the last thing I want to do is hit you with a massive
buzz kill about techno-relating just when you were about to text
message your friend about how much fun you're having with
this book. I just want to make sure you're aware of the bad, as
well as the good. And too many women I know have had a
healthy dose of both to simply ignore the topic altogether.

So let's wrap this chapter with a Myth vs. Reality list. This
way, we can ensure you're not focusing on unnecessary worries
and overlooking valid ones. The following facts come from illegal
hackers, corporate security companies, and victimized women—
all of whom wish to remain anonymous—so you're armed with
legit tips and lifestyle info about the culprits. Once you've digested the advice, you can carry on with your relationships more
assuredly than ever.

✉ **Myth:** Hackers are four-eyed geeks who are socially maladjusted introverts.

Reality: It takes a silver-tongued professional with charming people skills to pull off social engineering stunts; a con artist doesn't tout a pocket protector and degree in systems analysis to dupe you. Suits are much more persuasive, because they exude trustworthiness. However, some of the best hackers are geeks— and aren't afraid to flaunt it. Most are also self-aware enough to know they don't have the looks to pull off a heist, and as a result, have a front man that collects info for them. Insiders refer to these men as "Suaves," for obvious reason.

✉ **Myth:** Hacker geeks don't get laid.

Reality: Some hackers are having more interesting sex than you. According to an illegal hacker, the geek chic set LOVES sex. He adds: "Is it any wonder why the Web's first real industry was porn?" Point taken. I'm also told they tend to experiment with alternative lifestyles more than your usual population sample. My favorite source confided that one of the best hackers he's ever known was named Brian—and is now Brianna. When they were friends, Brian/Brianna had a girlfriend (another fanatic hacker) throughout his transgender journey. Together, they programmed simulations as coeds that the military still uses today. And yes, they're still an item.

✉ **Myth:** IT execs can't wait to tune into the next dramatic episode of your life on IM.

Reality: In general, IT and HR departments don't have time to comb your every word on their computers. However, this doesn't mean they don't implement systems that watch for language related to sexuality, finances, or violence. Because computers don't read context, words like "guaranteed" (because it implies a sales promise) or "blow up" (as in, bomb . . . not doll) are often flagged—and brought to a superior's attention. Comments that could be construed as terrorist-related threats, even if meant in jest ("I could just kill George Bush for his surveillance program!"), might invite an HR meeting—as would similar talk about your boss or coworkers. But in most cases, words don't carry weight unless you're already in legal trouble. Then, an official could pull a log as evidence.

⊠ **Myth:** My boss knows I spend six of my eight-hour day flirting online.
Reality: Doubtful, unless a jealous coworker snitches. Few companies employ timing programs, though these products do exist. For example, if your job is to write, the program would know if you spent ten hours using MS Word per week and twenty-five hours on IM. Your work ethic is now questionable. According to a recent study, 92 percent of employers conduct some form of workplace monitoring to ensure productivity and minimize liability. The newest breed of Employee Internet Monitoring (EIM) software can record keystrokes, sites visited, emails, windows opened, applications run, instant messages, print jobs, and capture actual screenshots of any computer used on the company network.

⊠ **Myth:** My biggest hacking concern should be email privacy.
Reality: Though you might type more words in an email, you

probably expose more of your uncensored soul over IM. Your guard is down, you're more forthright. The medium invites you to relax, chat, and exaggerate feelings you'd rather not have a hacker document. If you're logged-on in two places, your conversation will show—and you must be confident that you're talking about topics you would want others to see. Especially if you have work, home, and phone IM outlets. Ask yourself: Would I be totally humiliated or in really big trouble if someone else read this?

⊠ **Myth:** If I send my guy risqué photos, he'll tuck them under his pillow at night for safekeeping.
Reality: Be careful with posting photos on the Web, since hackers can easily post them on an alternative site and tarnish your image, reputation, and identity. Though this can happen to men, women are most often the victims. Ditto on the video front. If footage of your body smeared in Neapolitan ice cream lands in the wrong hands, you'll suffer more than infamy at your local Friendly's. These videos live a long life on the net—not to mention on thousands of hard drives.

⊠ **Myth:** Hackers need to know a variety of intimate details about your life before they can probe.
Reality: A good hacker can learn everything about you from two very basic pieces of info—your first and last name.

> **Hacker:** *Nice to meet you, Plain Jane. How old are you, and where are you from?*
> **Sucker:** *I'm 28, and I grew up in Miami.*
> Spooky, huh.

dear diary, today i met the cutest geek at kinkos . . .

As you might expect, hackers and con artists don't think of technology in the same terms as we do. In fact, their boundaries and definitions of what it even means to invade privacy are more expansive than anything we might conceive on our own. Rather than sum up an illegal hacker's ideas about all things tech, I'll let one tell you himself. Enter: TL Hacker (an alias, of course):

To me, fire is a technology. Paper is a technology. Computers and digital culture are just a recent development that people use to create and store information. A good hacker uses all 'technology' at their disposal to analyze a system. Can I hack paper? Of course! Da Vinci did it centuries ago and people still can't decipher his codes. So yes, da Vinci was a hacker. So was Jesus. Now that *was social engineering. . . .*

But back to paper. In my experience, women tend to journal and write entries more than men do. If there's ever a quick and easy way to get the skinny, a woman's personal papers may be the best windows to her soul. A poem is a piece of psyche just waiting to be analyzed."

So hide your mascara! Put tax forms through the shredder! And for heaven's sake, chuck that Hello Kitty diary in the nearest landfill! I'm kidding (sort of), but given that hackers and snoops consider every medium to be technology, you do need to be careful. There's a fine line between savvy awareness and fearful obsession. Only you know when you've crossed it.

07

>>CNTRL Z! CNTRL Z!
(or simply, damage control)

NO MATTER HOW MUCH YOU STUDY AND FOLLOW THIS book's recommendations, you're bound to still confuse an inter-action or misinterpret dialogue time and again. This is totally expected and in fact a good learning experience. Because there are so many factors at play (moods, language, visuals, memory, imagination, etc.) when you're techno-relating, nobody really expects you to perfect the art. In fact, regardless of how severely or often you misfire, techno-relating leaves room for a backup plan—a little spin, as PR mavens like to say.

As you know, technology and text trends outdate themselves on a daily basis, which means mishaps are actually built into the medium. The window for making a mistake based on an inability to keep up with changing technology is wide-open, and this is only compounded by human error (sending a note too soon, entering an incorrect text address, accidentally replying to all). As whizzes continue to create smart machines, their users' knowledge base can only keep up so quickly. No matter how sharp your learning curve or how patient your boyfriend, you, my dear, are only human. The best you can do when you flub up is do damage control for your missteps.

Now when I talk flubs, I'm covering the gamut: from sending a Cyranote without erasing your friend's name to berating your guy for suggesting a blow job over IM when his emoticon was really simulating surprise. And as any good spin doctor will tell you, the key to managing a mistake is to confront its central issue by immediately addressing the problem and sticking with talking points that either speak to or mask your snafu. Remember when Angelina poached Brad from his Hollywood marriage? Rather than deal with her sultry wiles, Angie's publicist choked the press with her Goodwill Ambassador efforts. That's brilliant spin.

Even when you're redirecting an audience's attention, which is a common offshoot of damage control, it's important to be as honest as you can, or else your mistakes will gather speed and debris like a desert tumbleweed. And considering that technomediums already demand that you think on your feet during quick repartee, it would be that much harder to explain away additional mistakes. There are, however, occasions in which I do endorse a little fib to save face—like those in which the recipient of an embarrassing message would never call out your blunder for fear of giving credence to the statement. Accidental insults and injuries are written at his ego's expense. Covering your tush isn't ethical, but in the name of maintaining a relationship, it is necessary. Technology can be a slippery slope, but you can only blame your Hotmail account for so much.

>>'fess up, sister

Whether you accidentally forward your guy an email chain full of personal problems or send a flirty text message intended for another man, you've got some explaining to do—and fast. At all costs, do not ignore it or wait for the angry (ouch), hurt (double ouch), or confused (ouch again) response. Just know that the deafening silence and nauseating shock that you feel upon realizing you fucked up is nothing compared to how he feels as the object of your fuck-up. It sucks to be you, but it sucks even harder to be him.

Though your instincts might tell you to play it cool, that's actually the worst MO you could have. Instead, it works to your benefit to behave like a spaz, because the best thing your guy can think is that you have too much on your mind to know what you're saying—and to whom. You're busy! You're scatterbrained! You didn't mean to call him John, when his name is Jay! As you prep to send a make-nice, be sure to do so via the same medium in which you committed the faux pas. If you send an errant email, don't apologize over the phone or IM. To move up the techno-relating hierarchy is to say you're so crippled with guilt that you're thinking way too hard about his feelings. Are you insane? Your goal is to demonstrate that you're in ten places at once, and you only have time to zap off a quick reply on a medium that's already at your fingertips. When you do, be sure to include a minor typo or three to reinforce that you're a walking train wreck—at least for the moment. And if your channel allows limited words or real-time pacing, prep ahead with a sharp one-liner or snappy response.

With this overarching tone, send a brief but sincere apology for your mistake. Your honesty, brevity, humor, and haphazard attitude will help him to blow off the situation. Promise to make it up to him. I recently heard a story about a couple that was not having sex because the man could have benefited from a little blue pill. He was mortified, she was frustrated—and the duo was on the verge of a breakup. Cut to the right mood on the right night, and his penis finally pulled through. The next morning, the woman was so happy that she meant to send her best friend a text message that said, "We're having sex!"—but accidentally sent it to her boyfriend (who would've been livid if he knew she was spreading the news). Instead, he was so thrilled himself that he simply typed back: "I know! And it's great!"

Life would be too easy if techno-relating mistakes always ended on such an up note. With every rule comes an exception, and the lighthearted spaz rule no longer applies if your gaffe has the potential to seriously upset. Name-calling, backstabbing, and mean-spirited gossip fall under this umbrella. So does any overt or lengthy sign of pursuing more men than him. If one (or all?) of these mistakes happen, you should first wait for his response—and then address his specific concern. No more, no less. What you may interpret as problematic, he might overlook, and there's no need to compound your troubles. Give yourself a good two hours to plan your strategy. When it comes to tone, take the apologetically self-deprecating route. Forget "I kid because I love." Now you kid because you don't love yourself. Play the "I'm miserable" card, and his own empathy will distract him. My friend Amy calls this "turning the beat around"—i.e., redirecting his attention toward how this situation reminds you of your own woes. In fact, whatever you've done says more about you than it does about him. And you're just so sorry. Because it's been that kind of week—make that, life. Before you know it, he'll be buying you drinks to discuss the unfair workload or overbearing mom that's caused you to be such a distressed airhead in the first place.

Whatever you do, avoid the retraction option available on some email systems as if it were your embarrassing aunt with a hunchback. These program-scripted memos only make things worse by telling a recipient that you have, indeed, sent them a mystery note that contains upsetting info—but nanny-nanny boo-boo, they'll never get to read it.

✒ oops! i did it again

Psychology 101 says there are no accidents, that every word you utter and every move you make has a subconscious motivation. So when you repeatedly say the unexpected to men whose feelings matter, you have to wonder if deep down inside you actually want your sweet pea to know how you privately feel. Is it really an accident that you wrote a diatribe about an ex's kissing skills, and sent it to your current beau who sucks face like a Hoover? Are you sure you didn't mean to tell his best friend you have a hot ass and aren't afraid to use it—on a mass email, no less? The next time you send a message, think twice! Not so much about your carelessness, but about your secret intentions. You could be standing in the way of getting what you want and actually saying what you mean. Now wouldn't that be a refreshing change, Ms. Subliminal?

>>and if you're on the receiving end?

Because nobody's perfect, there are times that you'll be on the receiving end of a mixed message. Eek, I know. Although you may want to fume, stomp, or even cry, your best bet is to stifle those instincts and focus on spin. This time, you're spinning your own feelings from annoyance to apathy. Because just like when your fingers slipped, you dreaded the response from the other person—and even if you confront the other person and they apologize profusely, everyone knows the explanation will be subtle bullshit. Techno-mishaps are the equivalent of talking about someone behind their back . . . and if eighth grade flashbacks are any indication, yelling at someone for hurting you first makes you look like a big dork. If the snafu has anything to do with your shortcomings, to confront the sender is to validate his words—not to mention, his power over your ego. The only way to assert your cool is to act like his text doesn't bother you. After all, it wasn't intended for your ears. He could be posturing for friends or buttering up a female coworker for a favor, right?

If, however, his message is disrespectful to a fault, then you must couple confrontation with action. To simply bark at him, but agree to a movie that night, gives him the thumbs-up to act without fear of repercussion. Take time to process his words before you let him rush to make nice. This recovery period is relative to both your relationship and the mistake. Visualize how you'd handle the situation if it went down off-line, and parallel your behavior. Naturally, you'd let some scenarios slide, others explode in private, and the worst invite a public hanging. When managing extreme anger and disappointment, your reaction should reflect how you pick battles in person.

>>from his screen to your psyche

It's one thing for me to describe a text-driven mistake and how to spin your response, but it is something entirely different to read how a guy might handle the situation when you are on the receiving end of his faux pas. Since my friend Colby is the king of techno-glitches, I asked him to send me an example of how he might do damage control for a nasty email. He wrote the below emails, as if he were to accidentally include me on a forward to his friend. Note how he spins his words online, but continues the make-nice in person. This way, his text spills into a consistent off-line rapport. Learn from his technique, while I decide whether to speak to him again.

```
To: gaberocks@innocentbystander.com
From: colbyisamanwhore@slanderouscad.com
Fwd: Please help with book
yo man,
that charlatan kristina g. interviewed me again.
what an eternal bore. i just try to humor her
(see below), to keep my own journalistic karma
on the up and up.
so we're meeting at the strippy later?
10:30? it's your turn to bring the rohypnol
bud deh.
peace,
colbs
```

To: colbyisamanwhore@slanderouscad.com
From: kristinatakesoffense@hmph.com
Re: Fwd: Please help with book
You just blew your Karma, kid. What the hell is
this?*

To: kristinatakesoffense@hmph.com
From: colbyisamanwhore@aol.com
Re: Fwd: Please help with book
i'm sorry you saw that (and that i sent it to you),
but i can explain: the note's not what it seems.
see how my insults are dripping with sarcasm?
that's how i talk about you. since i have a crush
on you, but gabe's super-tired of hearing me talk
about it in flowery ways, i recently decided to
talk about you only in less-than-flattering
terms, to sarcastically appease him. i actually
feel the opposite of what i wrote. and obv. the
part about strippers and roofies is a joke. i
don't associate with strippers.
can i make it up to you?**
xx.

**Colby says: If Kristina and I were hanging out, I'd have to go out on at least one nice date with her—my treat—to legitimize my spin. There'd be no other way. But after that, I could drop her like a hot potato. If she came back and said, "See! The way you ignore me now proves your email was NOT sarcastic in the first place," I would counter with: "It WAS sarcastic. I was interested in you, but our date made me realize we're simply too different." Ay yai yai . . .

*Kristina says: I wouldn't buy a word of Colby's rigmarole, but I'd give him a second chance over a free dinner. I wouldn't mention the email, but would realize the night doubles as a compatibility test for both of us. I'd judge him by his words, his perceived sincerity, and his pleated trousers. My instincts would be on high alert—as should be yours in do-over situations.

don't blame the messenger

As I've said from the start, you should admit to your mistake in the most genuine way possible. This doesn't include blaming your email provider, spam filter, postmaster, dead phone battery, or hovering boss for a slow response or tech-error. Take responsibility for neglectful replies. Nobody believes that your Yorkie can type eighty words a minute, anyway.

>>when "errors" work to your advantage

I'll never forget the time my friend Sarah sent her recent ex, a man with whom she hoped to reunite, an email that read:

```
Dear Seth,
Thanks for a great weekend in Fire Island.
Who knew an impromptu skinny dip could be so
much fun? You're right, silly
question. . . .
Let's do it again soon.
Miss you,
Sarah
```

Too bad Sarah's ex's name was *James*. But though her note appeared to be an innocent slip of the Send button, the truth is that her cunning email wiles were hard at work. You see, James is a lovely man who was also insanely jealous of Sarah's hunky pal Seth—all of which was info that Sarah used to her love life's advantage. There was no weekend away with Seth, no naked dip in the ocean. But five minutes after sending her note to "the wrong man," there *was* an unexpected call from Sarah: She rang James and calmly asked him to respect her privacy and delete the oops email she'd sent—which only made him open it faster (and after reading, ask her to dinner for a make-nice). Two years later, Sarah and James were married at the Rainbow Room—and Sarah's clueless, albeit adoring, new husband has yet to learn that Fate's hand was hardly responsible for the apparent snafu that prompted their reunion. It was Sarah's laptop that played Cupid.

Which is to say: The flip side of all this negative mishap talk is that you can actually make cyberspace's flawed rep work to your advantage. I don't love the idea of using it to invoke jealousy or create unnecessary drama on a regular basis, but every once in a while it doesn't hurt to remind your crush of just how funny, endearing, or in-demand you are. Realize, however, that sneaky manipulations are for fearless techno-pros who don't flinch at the prospect that there may be unpleasant consequences to their actions. If Sarah hadn't won James back, she'd have moved on to another man in her stockpile. Her eyes were fixed on the prize, but she was emotionally distant enough to deal with a lukewarm reply. To protect yourself, make sure your head's in the same place before you pull a stunt like hers. It's a devilish plan, but not a foolproof (or ethical) one.

>>damage control: the morning after

Since your online text should support and further your off-line relationships, let your favorite medium swoop in and save the day when you drop the ball in real life. No date is perfect, but some are certainly less perfect than others. If he moped when you mocked his rad trainers or shrugged out the door after an awkward sleepover, you now have the chance to fix what was fudged the night before. Though this move may do wonders for mending a fence, do not abuse the privilege. Slips and slides are part of dating, and can even be cute if you pull them off au natural. But repeat damage control after a date looks horribly self-conscious, and nobody likes an overly apologetic wimp. Save your text for worries that cause insomnia, not a laugh with friends.

So. Maybe you feel like a complete loser for neurotically cornering him about commitment issues? Or an impulsive prude for throwing water in his face when he squeezed your thigh? Control the damage by sending a message the following afternoon, after two p.m. but before his workday is over; any sooner implies that you can't wait to apologize. Mention the mistake, but couple it with a pleasant inside reference from the night before that counterbalances the effect your blunder has on his memory. You want your date to remember the evening as one during which you impressed him with your sake savvy, not one in which you asked if his package was the size of edamame. Pithy and succinct works best here. Because you don't want to draw too much attention to the mistake, tuck your apology into the middle of your message or save it for the end of an interaction so it reads as a near afterthought. You likely misspoke in a way that was more inappropriate than insincere. And if open and honest communication is the goal of every relationship, then you simply need to work that edit button a bit more swiftly. It's not so much what you said, but how or how soon you said it. Spin the scenario, and promptly move on. The longer you dwell on the rough patch, the longer he will too—and the extended focus can potentially outweigh the incident's importance.

08:

>>maintenance and updates

NO MATTER HOW COMPATIBLE YOU ARE WHEN TECHNO-relating, you can't expect your online and off-line chemistry to be in sync every time you're together. That would not only be impossible, it would be nauseating to those around you. Though it's easy to assume, this doesn't mean you're not attracted to each other. And if you're simpatico ninety-nine percent of the time, this also doesn't mean you'll spend eternity together with 2.5 kids and a white picket fence. So where does that leave you?

Online and off-line compatibility takes self-evaluation to another level. Because you're bonding on two very intense planes, it's important that you really evaluate your relationship as it exists in both arenas—and how you fit each other's needs. Technologies change, people change, and the way that one affects the other is constantly in flux. If you use technology as a primary communication tool, then your relationship's growth may evolve in tandem. Even in the most fulfilling relationships, it's all too likely that you'll misunderstand your guy's text or he'll misinterpret yours at some point—just as you would each other's words in real life. We've talked about how to avoid the online/off-line language disconnect so you can put your real self forward. Yet no communication agenda is ever perfect, and if it were, there'd be no need for therapists, NLP, or Oprah. Similarly, you can't expect the interactive details of your online/off-line relationship to play out as predictably as it does on-screen. The secret to real happiness with your match requires more emotional depth than any smiley face or blog entry could express.

So if you're casually dating a few good men or hopelessly devoted to one in particular, you need to learn how to maintain and update your love life like you would any high-quality gadget. Your relationship is prone to glitches, loose wires, and even the occasional breakdown. It requires regular maintenance and updates for easy operation and impressive resale value, if need be. So give yourself the TLC you deserve and put your own interests first.

Techno-relating both inspires great relationships and helps enrich them. But you need to know how to find the perfect balance between behavior, communication, and self-awareness to fluidly transfer your character from one encounter to the next.

>>stop looking for signs

Let's say you spent the day snuggling with your guy in the park. You're stunning, he's complimentary. You laugh, you talk, and in your mind, you couldn't connect better if you were conjoined twins. But when you send him a text message on your way home to thank him for the afternoon, you're met by cyber silence. What the what? Ten minutes ago under a blossoming cherry tree, he played with your pinky toe and professed his adoration. Now your mind leaps to whether you'll ever see him again. When exactly did this online/off-line disjuncture happen?

Here's the thing: It didn't. Relax, you two had fun. The above is not only an example of exaggerated expectations, but also proof that online/off-line rapport is not seamless. Logically speaking, how could it be? Even the best wordsmiths can't craft text in the exact timing and tone as you'd ideally imagine it—and then mirror the very same attention in person. And vice versa! That would mean if he's more emotionally open after a glass of wine, he'd have to summon the nerve to gush feelings over email. Or if he sent rapid-succession text messages, it would be a sign that he'd stalk you silly. Although a simple response might prove you're on the same page, he may also feel that he's already proven his affections in person. Maybe he simply smiled to himself when he received the note, and thought a formal reply would be overzealous, superfluous, or unable to live up to the real encounter. The point is, you can do your best to communicate a consistent personality and tone . . . but do expect a few intentions to get lost in translation when they're actualized. Whether we like it or not, this is yet another snag in connecting via a medium to which no rules were previously attached. Even if you take the lead according to my advice, it will take your partner more than a minute to catch up.

What's most important is that you recognize how you feel

most comfortable when you techno-relate and when you're in person—and put yourself in situations that summon these emotions. If you like the person you are over IM but feel awkward over email, limit your mediums. If you're most confident making plans on the phone, and sending a thank-you via Web cam, have a ball. Your personality traits that push through the strongest are what determine chemistry, so don't multitask on channels that don't bring out your best. Any relationship is a process of gathering information, and you're doing so in two very different and intense ways. To negate a connection simply because of an inconsistency in those two channels is premature and unnecessary. Evaluate how you feel in both online and off-line scenarios—and if one outweighs the other, consider how you might tweak your talk and decide if the relationship is right for you.

When you sense a sudden divide, it's seldom a result of chemistry drain, since you've built momentum thus far. It's more likely that how you're techno-relating isn't best for your specific personalities. Be confident and consistent about the person you put out into the world—and don't think for a second that steady means flat or myopic. There are so many complex elements which create your multifaceted self that you shouldn't let a medium define your personality, which then helps determine chemistry. Just as you would in real life, actively create scenarios in which you shine. You'd never suggest a ski trip if you're a beach bunny, so why send a curt note over text if you enjoy a verbose email? Flaunt every one of your attributes—from honest, to sensitive, to high-brow, to goofy—in the best online and off-line situations possible. Try not to speed-dial your mom if he doesn't respond in kind, but do expect him to acknowledge your message in some fashion. Anything less is poor form, even for the most obviously inept.

>>developing QT with your cutie

Because so many tech-centric couples move at extreme paces, they often find it difficult to carve out alone time without their co-dependent gadgets when romance really brews. And as technology grows increasingly progressive, the more challenging it becomes to make live interactions a norm and not a novelty. Why see each other four days a week when your video phone can chop that to two? Why talk for hours on the museum steps when you volleyed on email between meetings?

Because real relationships happen between real people—and techno-relating is a supplement to, not substitute for, a solid bond. If you want your relationship to thrive, make sure that neither you nor your guy dismisses the crux of what brought you together in the first place: common interests, mutual friends, similar goals, like-minded values, comparable sex drives, and so on. If your opposites attracted, then exploit those differences to their most satisfying ends. But this time, try it without your tech in hand.

Once you're in a dating comfort zone, you may notice that the fury with which you first techno-related will die down. And if he's not a total dating dunce, he'll begin to supplement other modes of affection beyond the shiny, blinking, beeping kind. It was easy and convenient to enchant you over IM or email, but once your couplehood is off and bonking, techno-relating becomes a way of maintaining your relationship and not necessarily solidifying it. Your messages will become less frequent, more casual, and increasingly direct—and these are all good signs.

Such indicators show that you've both graduated to a new interpretation of technology based on convenience and purpose that's different from the hierarchy that opened the book. In your early courtship stages, the technology hierarchy was about how to best graduate to the next level of get-to-know-you. But when you're in a more secure relationship, technology becomes yet another way to track each other down. The scale becomes horizontal, and each method has a reason. And yes, the once elusive phone conversation will become a norm. You'll spend more time chatting into your cells because it's no longer intimidating to hear each other's voices—and your stutter factor has gone way down.

✍ will he ever just leave me alone?

Now that techno-relating is but one way to reach out, our scale has literally flipped on its side. When you're comfortable in your relationship, connections are no longer about progressing to the next level, but about using devices to stay close. Previously, the ladder extended the meander to your first few dates, but once you're an item, techno-relating plays a different role in your life. Though the scales vary from one relationship to the next, most will now look like this:

✉ **Personal emails:** Use only one of these to relay private information. Suddenly, you care very much about whether his assistant and boss have access to your smutty emails and sappy e-cards.

⊠ **Work email:** Unless you respond to a note from him first, you'll seldom use this address. It's easier to hit reply than to open a new message window.

⊠ **Instant Message:** Use this to retrieve a quick answer, make a brief connection, or rant about your mom or a coworker: *Where's the party tonight? Are we ordering in or are you cooking? Have I got a story for you. . . .*

⊠ **Text message:** Use when determining the five W's of meetup: *Who's coming? What should I wear? Where are we going? When do we show? Why didn't you make a reservation?* Also ideal for quick sentiments: *I miss you* or *Buy condoms?* sure can make the day fly.

⊠ **Voice mail:** Use in conjunction with any of the above to contact your guy or leave a long-winded message with specific info. Sometimes, the simple act of calling, hanging up, and tagging him with a "missed call" message is all you need to prompt action.

⊠ **Phone call:** Use your cell when you need to emotionally connect, hear his voice, and remember why you're not on IM with your ex.

>>once you're on the same page . . .

. . . you might actually benefit from deviating from techno-relating. Because you've both spent so much time chatting online, and you already spend hours in front of your computer for work, happy couples agree that a handwritten letter or clever Post-it note breaks through the clutter. All things spontaneous will charm affections, solicit smiles, and warm hearts.

Although you've totaled impressive hours online, I'll assume you haven't forgotten how to intrigue a man without the help of spell-check. And since you two are so immersed in technology, one of the best ways to show him how much you care is to surprise him with what he least expects off-line. In our techno-savvy world, something that would have had little effect twenty years ago, like sending a store-bought card, now leaves twice the impression. It requires effort to choose the right message and lick a tacky stamp. And on a lazy day, it can be a long hard trek to the mailbox.

Here, a few counterintuitive tricks that stray from tech and make your sugar smile.

✉ **Tech Says:** Short and sweet is a powerful force.
So Now You: Show you're just as capable of nonirritating exposition as Jane Eyre.
Here's How: Send him a love letter, complete with a whiff of lavender perfume.

✉ **Tech Says:** Online courtship is convenient.
So Now You: Really put yourself out to impress him.
Here's How: Plan an entire day around his likes, not yours. Even if this means sitting through a sports event . . . with a smile . . . surrounded by grunting men . . . stone-cold sober. (I just got chills.)

✉ **Tech Says:** Reveal your assets and flaws, pronto. Memorize those talking points!
So Now You: Become the mystery woman he's never met.

Here's How: Reserve the corner banquette at a dark, shadowy cabaret. Candlelight is your friend.

✉ **Tech Says:** Control your expectations.
So Now You: Throw caution to the wind.
Here's How: Let him plan a day of unforeseen treats.
Cheers to the unexpected!

✉ **Tech Says:** It's okay to be selfish with your personal space.
So Now You: Learn to coexist as a unit, rather than a voice or message.
Here's How: Spend a weekend together at a cozy B&B and share a bar of soap.

✉ **Tech Says:** Tease him as much as you want.
So Now You: Actually follow through with your taunts.
Here's How: I'll let you take it from here. . . .

>>save as . . .

REGARDLESS OF WHETHER YOU'VE SNAGGED ONE special man, a few delicious choices, or heaps of doozies with potential, at some point you'll want to stop juggling your options. I know it's oh-so-flattering to have various gentlemen callers, especially when each brings something fresh to your dynamic—who knew how much you'd enjoy flying to Paris, simply for brunch? Or that a quick Boggle challenge would lead to becoming an overnight etymology sensation?—but whittle down your most delicious prospects because hanging out with so many men at once dulls your sensibilities. Forget the moral implications of doling out kisses to multiple men, shagging your best two options, or leading them all to think that they have a shot at being your main squeeze. I'm no saint—and I don't expect you to be either. But you can't possibly give all of yourself to one person when there are multiples floating about in your dating queue. Even if tartlets hone this skill on reality TV, it doesn't mean you should. You ultimately want to connect with someone special, and that's a really hard task when you're sharing various aspects of yourself with lots of men.

If one lover is exceptionally empathetic, you might not expect your other options to fill that need; if another is extremely sexual, you may not even crave action from someone who's intellectually stimulating. Regardless of whether you online date, techno-relating still has an uncanny ability to forge immediate closeness with new men—whether they're friends, peers, or acquaintances. For many women, flirting has become second nature thanks to the casual attitude that accompanies new tech. The massive upshot is that although you don't plan to date all of these guys, you'll be able to better distinguish the qualities that suspiciously raise an eyebrow or happily turn your head. Between the men you've dated and those on the periphery, you'll have a clearer understanding of what you want, expect, and need from a partnership. You'll know what qualities make you smile, cringe, freak, and claw like a wildcat. Of course, it's impossible to expect all of the facets you seek to be embodied in one man—but having so many pass in and out of your life will help set your priorities straight through example alone.

When it's time to throw down the dating gavel, listen to your gut as much as that ringing cell or beeping inbox. At one time, it might have been enough to assess how you felt when one sent you online animated shorts or another threw you down on a queen-size bed in Bloomie's linens department. But now, you have your in-person and techno-lives to consider when choosing Mr. Right. Obviously in-person rapport far outweighs online affinity, though the modern world has done a pretty good job at ensuring that the two are inextricably linked.

>>you can click it. but can you take it?

So you're in lust, love, or ready to move on from existing affairs. Chances are, you have at least one lingering interest or romantic straggler vying for a position in your heart that he'll never assume. He's a great guy, but there's something about the way he eyes your sister's rump or slurps milk from his cereal bowl that nudges your conscience into thinking that he's not quite for you. Don't tell me: You feel more than a bit responsible for leading him down a path and ditching him at the crossroad, right? But as I've said before, techno-relating lends itself to a rotating door of online mates, casual relationships, and meaningless flirtations. And because the mediums are so different, each lends itself to various endings. In some cases, it can be downright liberating. In others, these have emotional ramifications that can be hard on both you and your leftovers. So how's a girl to deal?

Thanks to the burgeoning impact of hook-up culture, starter marriages, and fuck buddies, romantic rejection has become easier to swallow. It's not so much that we've grown more sturdy backbones or spent more hours on a leather couch (although both may be true), but that we've learned to accept what was once an intolerable concept: Grandma was wrong. There isn't someone for everyone. In fact, techno-relating has taught us that there are someones (plural) for everyone. With enough resources, communication devices, and knowledge about qualities that vibe with your personality, you can conquer the dating world head-on or pelvis-first. The term "rejection" isn't as quickly equated with the words "disposable" or "consolation prize" as they once were.

I'm not saying it doesn't hurt a guy when he's passed over as your #1, or vice versa—because it really, really can. And if it happens often enough, the discarded one may start to feel like a walking callus. But because techno-relating forces vulnerability, challenges commitment, and thrives on frequent self-evaluation, I can't help but think that more good than bad results from missed connections. I've never bought the cliché that everything happens for a reason. But I do believe that what doesn't kill you makes you stronger. And unless some Match.com addict is after you with a machete for playing his heartstrings like a maestro, I see only fortitude in your relationship's gorgeous future. The details just need a little tweaking, that's all.

I've found that unsuccessful romances, based in technology, actually open the door to compartmentalized friendships, which work really well in our fast-paced and niche society. If you met online, you've likely based at least one date around a shared interest—and all of the others are printed before you, ready to be tailored to your specific needs. So, you smeared a guy for his mother issues during touch football with your friends, and you all decided that he's not the best boyfriend material. But the way he stuffs a chicken and orders cavatelli in a perfect Italian accent speaks to your foodie instincts. Though things won't work out romantically, it doesn't mean you can't plow through the Michelin Guide together. If you met another man on a blind date or through other off-line means, you know at least two dates-worth (come on, everyone deserves two dates) of stats about his hobbies, career, family, etc. And if he absolutely adores kids and you need a plus-one to a family barbecue? I think your solution's obvious!

As you get to know each man better based on his interests and your needs, lovely friendships are bound to bloom. And who knows? Just because you weren't hot for how he circled his tongue around the lid of a peanut butter jar doesn't mean one of your single girlfriends won't be. Or that he won't want to continue your relationship in a new way. Give him up to two weeks to brush off his ego from your gentle blow, and then drop him a message via whatever medium he likes most. Get right to the point in your note: You have two tickets to opening night at the theater, and would he like to join you? Don't use the f-word (that's "friend," you gutter-mind), but do tell him you're seeing someone if he asks. If he doesn't, make it abundantly clear that you're not WITH him, though you're with him: Compliment the lead's forearms, the bartender's rear, suggest he say hi to the redhead that's looking his way between acts. He'll get the point.

baby, you're the IM of my life. . . .

You know the qualities you desire in a boyfriend, friend, or playmate. And so far, technology has helped secure a few options. But when it comes to choosing The One, you won't seek clarity by tallying who sent the most text messages or ranking relationship pros and cons on an Excel spreadsheet. To determine just how much you like a guy, it helps to recognize the degree of urgency with which you want to see him next. So why not compare your options to speedy-delivery mediums? This may just help suss out the depth of your new

love. Or not . . . but it's kind of a fun metaphor. (Urgency rat-
ings work on a scale of one to five; five being the highest.)

Is He . . .

✉ **An Email:** You let sentiments pile up before you respond
on your watch. What's the rush?

Urgency Rating: ***

✉ **An Instant Message:** You love to banter at break-neck
speed, even if your partner is demanding.

Urgency Rating: ****

✉ **A BlackBerry:** You feel compelled to check it, like a love
addict in need of a hit.

Urgency Rating: *****

✉ **A Cell Phone:** Maybe you answer . . . or maybe you banish
the losers straight to voice mail.

Urgency Rating: **

✉ **An Online Community Profile:** With few exceptions, text
is more style than substance. Yet somehow, you're still
hooked on the glitz.

Urgency Rating: *****

✉ **A Text Message:** Incoming! You smile. You read. You reply
according to feelings and intentions.

Urgency Rating: ****

✉ **A Video Phone:** How can you resist a guy's abs in your
face? You can't reply fast enough.

Urgency Rating: *****

>>when hitting send is hard to do

It's time to decide which dudes are worth storing, which belong in the recycling bin, and which get deleted from your life altogether. We've already talked about the happy medium of turning flings into compartmentalized friends—but what about the rest of the lot? The men who aren't right for you now, but might eventually grow into their ears or gain life perspective after earning their first million? Or the men who date your coworkers under an online alias, not to mention vote Republican and refuse to floss? What about them? You have some serious sifting to do.

Let's start with the recyclables. They may be soda cans and beach glass today, but give them five years and they'll be cozy fleece jackets and sparkling jewelry. Unfortunately, these men aren't visibly stamped with the universal "reuse me" triangle, but it won't take long for you to separate potential keepers from disposable trash. They're men with whom you have a connection, but who lack maturity or wisdom or like-minded sensibilities. Once they've moved out of Mom's house or been fired from their first stable job, they'll gain the life experience that gives them the edge you already have. If the problem isn't that they've yet to fully ripen, perhaps they need more time to play around before they can commit to one person. This brand dates at a dizzying rate, and although you're both convinced that you're destined to be together, the man needs more time to sow his oats. Let him. Better to have him buy you fancy dinners with a full awareness of where you both stand, than to secretly hope that as he dates other women, he'll ultimately pick you. When you're ready, decisions are easier to make when your attachment feels more comfortable.

In all back-burner cases, believe in your connection—but know that you have to live in the meantime. If Life wants you to reconnect in a real way, it'll happen. Until then, let recyclable men pay for a boozy night on the town once a month. That's just enough time for you to become a faint but pleasant memory— until one enchanted evening, he feels a sudden jolt from your fabulousness and insists you reunite. The important thing to remember is that recyclable men must make you feel, at all times, like you are a very rare find. Be selective about who you drop into this bin! Be sure that he views you how those closest to you do, even if one of you isn't ready for the other. Be sure that he adds to your life, and doesn't subtract or flatline it. Be sure to build your rapport and gather information on each other. At the very least, you'll have a substantial friendship for a very long time.

Now for those who deserve the old heave-ho, quiet your conscience and don't devote too much what-if headspace to someone you're leaving behind. I don't mean to sound callous, but if you've decided that you're not a good match, then you should be excited to move on. Too many women stay in relationships because they feel bad about how the breakup will hurt or affect their partner. Spare me. The person whose romantic happiness matters most is very obviously you. And if a man isn't right for you, then the only thing you're guilty of is looking out for yourself.

Although technology has played a huge role in your relationship thus far, I definitely don't suggest you break up via any medium that requires a charger. Sure, you used tech to jump-start your relationship, but you were in the process of growth, winding up for what you hoped would be the start of something special. But now that you know otherwise, your breakup should be a clean cut. It's laden with heavy emotion and self-reflection, even if you both know it's for the best. Dumping a man over text message or even a long-winded email is not only passive-aggressive, but downright cruel. It's a one-two punch—without the benefit of reading his response. Body language can help soften the blow if you're trying to let him down gently, or if he's a total SOB, seeing him being a jerk in person can help you exit without guilt.

What's more, I think it's imperative that when leaving a person's love life, you offer him as much info about your feelings with as much honesty as you have the strength to muster. Such a sensitive transaction simply can't occur over technology. Even via Web cam or DV-cam, pixilated tears and a computer screen create an inappropriate distance. No matter how personal you are, the same tech that once produced exaggerated intimacy now generates immeasurable detachment. Don't let him think you're careless or are opting for the easy way out of a mess. Your dumpee already knows you have a computer; now show him you have a heart.

>>then again, every rule has an exception— or four

Make no mistake: I think it's hurtful to use technology as your go-between when you're ending a relationship. However, that's when you've spent time and made real memories together. If you've only been on two freaky dates, learned he was cheating, or heard he spread venomous rumors behind your back, then by all means, dump the bastard over tech and bcc your friends.

Of course, those aren't the only reasons to can him with visible indifference. Unplug if . . .

⊠ He booty texts you, before you've even met in person.

⊠ He asks to be reimbursed for his long-distance calling plan—
   and you live next door.

⊠ You have more interesting email chats with his mother than
   you do with him.

⊠ He replies-all to a family invitation to watch Halley's
   Comet . . . with a jpeg of his hairy Full Moon.

afterword:

>>a match made in cyberspace

NOW THAT I'VE ARMED YOU WITH A FINE SET OF techno-relating skills, use them on fine men worth squeezing into your busy agenda and double bed. You've learned the importance of creating rapports that glow as brightly on-screen as they do over a picnic lit by tea lights. So don't neglect your standards as your newfound skills invite a flood of anxious suitors. Real romance is underscored by strong rapport and open communication. And with so many tech devices in your life, plus a keen awareness of how to manipulate them, your chances of hitting the L-mark have considerably increased in only 162 pages.

But please, do us both a favor and customize the advice in this book. Although these tips have done wonders for the love lives of people I know, the truth is that I don't know you. Communication, relationships, and technology are three very personal topics. Are you more brazen or shy than *The Joy of Text* assumes? Then pull back at some parts, and push forward at others. If you're more tech-savvy than the average gal, earmark key chapters and make copies of the rest for your lonely sister. Tech is the playground for ingenuity and reinvention. So take advantage, and do a little redefining yourself. Before you know it, a fantastic guy will chase your lead—and you'll soon speak the same language while your iTunes croon in the background.